Scratchings on the Wall

(Selected Lyrics: 1982-2009)

Scratchings on the Wall

(Selected Lyrics: 1982-2009)

by
Dave Winans

iUniverse, Inc.
New York   Bloomington

Copyright © 2009 by Dave Winans

All rights reserved. No part of this book may be used or reproduced by any means, graphic, electronic, or mechanical, including photocopying, recording, taping or by any information storage retrieval system without the written permission of the publisher except in the case of brief quotations embodied in critical articles and reviews.

Photography by Vicki deLilla.

iUniverse books may be ordered through booksellers or by contacting:

iUniverse
1663 Liberty Drive
Bloomington, IN 47403
www.iuniverse.com
1-800-Authors (1-800-288-4677)

Because of the dynamic nature of the Internet, any Web addresses or links contained in this book may have changed since publication and may no longer be valid. The views expressed in this work are solely those of the author and do not necessarily reflect the views of the publisher, and the publisher hereby disclaims any responsibility for them.

ISBN: 978-1-4401-5760-8 (sc)
ISBN: 978-1-4401-5761-5 (ebook)

Printed in the United States of America

iUniverse rev. date: 07/13/09

Special thanks to the musicians who put up with me and all the people who put me up: Tim Barney, Michael Botos, Fred Buffum, Chris Chapman, Ric Craig, Hugh Drescher, Tom Ernst, Tobe Kniffin, Paul Hitchon, John Laprey, George Markam, Joel O'Lari, Chip O'Lari, Chris Rose, Rob Schmoyer, Doug and Joan Jakobs, the Griscoms and Wagners, Fred Loney and family, Caroline, Sister Mary, Wesley especially for the trip to Rochester, Dad and Mom, Gran, Nan, Melissa and Pete, the crew at Crescent Street, Valerie, Mike Green, Jake Dunnell, the Rev, Mr. G., Hugh Ogden, Miss G., Sandy Richardson, Sharon, MoJo and my one true love, Miss Vick.

"May God bless and keep you always."

Contents

Introduction 1

Woodshedding: 1982-1984 3

From Dog Beach to Crescent Street: 1985-1988 27

Woodbox and Harp: 1989-1992 75

Splitting Time: 1993-2000 105

Fiddle Me A River: 2001-2009 127

Afterthoughts and Acknowledgements 167

"My son, it's most important,"
My father said to me,
"To put your faith in what you feel
And not in what you see."

from "Lemon Tree"
(an old folk song)

Scratchings on the Wall *first appeared as a self-produced bound collection of song lyrics with commentary back in 1993. This abridged and revised edition brings my efforts at lyric writing up to date. It is a curious thing, perhaps, but it might, on some level, speak to you as Ralph Ellison's* Invisible Man *did to me back in the days of my impressionable youth.*

My family and friends will tell you that I've always been lost in thoughts and dreams, often ignoring what is going on around me. This may explain why I feel less equipped to write stories or a novel. I'm more of a poet by nature, though I consider these lyrics my art work, not necessarily my poetry. In the past I've claimed otherwise, but now I know not what to define it but more what it is — my awkward attempts to express myself in words. The lyrics sometimes come first, but more often I fiddle around with the guitar and think of a mood certain melodies would help establish. So I readily admit these words are missing their other half, those sound paintings people such as Joel, Rob, Fred, John, Paul and Montana Tom helped me make more complete. But the words are what I wish to share with you at this time.

Music creeps through walls and arguments and at least makes your problems tolerable. As a kid I used to listen to Dylan on my daddy's lap and my mom playing show tunes on the piano. I learned as much from the folk singers' words as I did from the poetry taught in school. I also made this magical discovery of r & b singers and 50's rock 'n roll when I'd break curfew at boarding school just to listen to the mighty Wolfman's radio show on Sunday nights. Gospel, rock and blues all moved me. As long as it was either raw or genuine. So much is product. Hearing John Prine's Bruised Orange *convinced me Mark Twain and Woody Guthrie's spirits were still around. Dylan's* Blood On the Tracks *played like a soundtrack to my own parents' divorce. At the time, ol' Chuck Berry's "Reelin' An Rockin'" spoke more directly to me than anything Shakespeare had to say. I'd eventually read Kerouac and Keats, Virginia Wolfe and Faulkner, but I did that more out of obligation. I listened to Neil Young and Van Morrison because I had the desire to do so. Writing my own lyrics wasn't so much a reaction as it was an extension to all that.*

This revised edition concludes with some tributes to writers and musicians whose own stories moved me to pay my respects. I also tip my hat and offer thanks to Jonathan Richman, Ani DiFranco, and Patti Smith who inspired me to always be myself and do what I felt was truly right.

Woodshedding: 1982-1984

Living in the woods of Salem, Connecticut was where I first started making lyric writing my chosen art. I was staying in the attic of this house my stepmother used to own, down by Gardiner Lake. Chopped wood for the stove and paid one thirty-five a month to a sweet woman named Barbara. She had a German shepherd called Jason. I lived there two winters and wrote a lot of dumb songs. "Tuesday Unemployment Line Rag" and "Runaway" came from this time in the early winter of '82. I knew it wasn't my calling in life, but it was something I had to answer to.

I was working at this alternative high school that shut down in January leaving me free to bowl a couple times a week and every other Tuesday collect the huge sum of a hundred and sixty-five dollars. It gave me a chance to get more intimate with a friend's Yamaha guitar and my mom's old Gibson. Though I never progressed beyond a certain illiterate rhythmic knowledge, I kept at it whenever I attempted to express myself with words.

That summer I took a job for the fall in south Florida. I was about to go on a journey into the world of playing music with other people. First there was Frank Wagner who knew a couple John Denver songs. He gladly played along to my comical first attempts at the "Unemployment Line" song. It was during this time that I wrote "Sister Mary" about my precious friend and sister Molly. Frank's wife Pat used to breastfeed her kid while we played so she ended up in the song as well. "Westerly Still Life" came from some lonely night in my one room apartment. Nostalgia doesn't always mean sentimentality. I found that out writing these songs.

Sister Mary

*Mother feeding life to her child
As the wars come and go.
I've got memories of tomorrow,
Busted dreams, a broken home.*

*And I don't know about the weather,
The joy to come or the pain.
We just might get some sunshine;
We just might get more rain.*

*Sing to me, Sister Mary
Sing to me of the dawn
Follow the road you believe in
Before the daylight's gone.*

*You might find yourself a beggar
Who holds the key to your heart.
Some find the answer in the moonlight,
Some chase a shooting star.*

*I've seen too much to remember,
All that's left to comfort me
Is this old coat full of holes in it
And memories of what could be.*

*Sing to me, Sister Mary
Sing to me of the dawn
Follow the road you believe in
Before the daylight's gone.*

Westerly Still Life

Funny but it seems to me
You and I have been here before.
I could swear I heard you say back then
You weren't coming back here anymore.
After all those years of loneliness
You finally found your long lost friend,
And now you look uncertain
Watching the night return again.

And the darkness rolls
Across a thousand dreams unknown

From those summers by the water
When we were young and still believed
That everything we wanted
Would turn out to be all that we'd need,
To wedding vows and first-time jobs
We never thought would last that long,
And the feeling for the one you love
Like the silence of the wind it just blows on.

And the darkness rolls
Across a thousand dreams unknown

*Listening to the rain come down
As we crawl out of our bed.
Yes, our daily deeds of decency
Go unnoticed like countless words unsaid.
Sitting in our Ford one night
On the empty streets of our hometown,
Listening to the radio
For those old songs that hardly ever
Come around.*

*And the darkness rolls
Across a thousand dreams unknown*

Tuesday Unemployment Line Rag

*The unemployment line is a very fine line
And I done served my time on the unemployment line*

*I been laying 'round since I been laid off,
And I just can't shake this horrible cough.
I do say Lord I've been better off,
But I don't blame the system or my boss.
She was just doing her job.*

*"Well tell me, son, how does it feel?"
"Well I tell ya, Dad, it feels quite real.
At eighty bucks a week it's a great steal.
I just had to cut out one of my meals,
No dinner."*

*Now everyone in line they never look around,
And the unemployment center's in the middle of town.
Everybody sees you going in and coming out,
And Willie Nelson's singing in the background.
He's lucky he can sing for his supper.*

*Well every other Tuesday you can find me
Standing in that line for half an hour usually.
Folks are friendly there 'cause they're happy to see
They're not the only ones hit by the economy.
You know what they say about misery.*

*Yeah, the unemployment line is a very fine line
And I done served my time on the unemployment line.*

Runaway

*Debbie left home when she was twelve
'cause her daddy used to beat her up,
Every morning he apologized,
And every night he came home drunk.
Debbie's still a pretty young girl,
That doesn't bother her tricks,
She dreams of Robert Redford's eyes
while some guy gets his kicks.*

*There's no tomorrow just today
Hey, hey, hey for the runaway*

*Danny left home to hitchhike west,
One night he got into a van.
He didn't know what was going down
'till he was raped by a middle-aged man.
Danny was ashamed and he wanted to cry,
He couldn't face his world back home.
He did some dealing just to get by,
Now he walks the streets alone.*

*There's no tomorrow just today
Hey, hey, hey for the runaway*

Linda left home when her parents divorced,
She went back, she was only ten.
Then Linda's stepfather made her sleep with him,
A year later she was gone again.
Now Linda's got no place to go,
Some nights she sleeps in the park,
But who knows maybe someday baby
She'll be a famous movie star.

There's no tomorrow just today
Hey, hey, hey for the runaway

This Train's Bound to Roll

I'm goin' back
To Colorado
Where the river
Still flows.
I'm goin' home
To find Katy,
I never lost my memory.

And this train's
Bound to roll
And it rolls
Through the day,
I'm goin' home,
I feel alone,
But hey, hey, hey,
The ride's okay.

I was twenty,
Now I'm twenty-three,
I've seen Broadway,
That's not for me.
The change was good,
I got by,
Now I need to see
The open sky.

*And this train's
Bound to roll
And it rolls
Through the night,
I'm goin' home,
I feel alone,
But hey, hey, hey,
The ride's all right.*

*I see the station
Waiting up ahead,
Needs new paint
Like it did the day
I left.
Colorado sun
Make me smile,
I'm feelin' good,
Might stay awhile.*

*And this train's
Bound to roll
And it rolls
Through the dawn,
I'm goin' home,
I feel alone,
But hey, hey, hey,
The train rolls on.*

Wesley's Blues

I'm the troubled kid, I'm the rebellious one,
I've got no great cause I'm just the no good son,
If that's what I am then that's what I am so be it.

I never finished school, I caused all kinds of grief,
I got mischievous eyes, but I aint no thief,
I guess you could say I just never learned how to fit.

But now I'm rockin' an' a-reelin'
And I just got on this feelin' it's all right.

I worked for awhile on a cruise line ship,
I pulled in the lines and learned how to rig,
Long hours, low pay, a journeyman's work.

There was no reason for me to quit,
I just got tired and decided to split,
I don't like my feet when they begin to hurt.

But now I'm rockin' an' a-reelin'
And I just got on this feelin' it's all right.

I'm goin' to Montana, I hear it's mighty green,
There's all these places I never seen,
It's summertime and right now I can feel the breeze.

I'm still young, I got a long way to go,
Think I'll head out and go down the road,
I got no place right now I got to be.

But now I'm rockin' an' a-reelin'
And I just got on this feelin' it's all right.

Salem

Old Charlie jumped in his car
And went off to find a shooting star.
The old coot sure likes to drive,
Also likes time off from his wife.

Living's lonely in the country
Unless you've found someone worth loving

Sammy Pyle's the best plumber in town,
A decent man with his feet on the ground,
But poor Sammy drinks too much,
After ten beers he's out of touch.

Living's lonely in the country
Unless you've found someone worth loving

Alice works in the grocery store,
You always see her sweeping up the floor.
She's got three kids, two dogs and a cat,
Her husband left her just like that.

Living's lonely in the country
Unless you've found someone worth loving

See your neighbors chopping up wood,
Warm gestures like a wave are understood.
A lot of great people in this town,
A lot of great people just aint been found.

Living's lonely in the country
Unless you've found someone worth loving

The Ballad of Tom Rivers

Well his name was Tom Rivers.
He spent his life on the lam.
He had a cold-blooded heart
And a fist for a hand.
He never looked for trouble,
It'd been there all along.
He never did no right
'cause all he knew was wrong.

He got a bullet in his head,
And his blood was on the street,
Just like the woman he'd slept with,
She got it in the sheets.
Just another sad story, brother,
You'll be watching on TV.
The shame aint how he died,
And that don't seem right to me.

I sing the blues of democracy
Of the land of opportunity
Where everybody can be brave and free
And they don't know what to do
No, they don't know what to do

Tommy left three kinds behind
With a wife who was sixteen.
They lived off candy bars and Coke,
It was not a pretty scene.
Her name was Lucy Rivers,
She got picked up more than once,
Then she found out she was with a child,
More trouble in eight months.

*I sing the blues of democracy
Of the land of opportunity
Where everybody can be brave and free
And they don't know what to do
No, they don't know what to do*

*Well Tommy's kids grew up to be
Three kids without a dad,
One of them turned out okay,
The other two went bad.
Jimmy's in jail charged with rape,
Tommy Jr. pushes drugs,
Mary reads the Bible
And sings of God's love*

*I sing the blues of democracy
Of the land of opportunity
Where everybody can be brave and free
And they don't know what to do
No, they don't know what to do*

*Well his name was Tom Rivers,
He spent his life on the lam.
He had a cold-blooded heart
And a fist for a hand.
He never looked for trouble,
It'd been there all along.
He never did no right
'cause all he knew was wrong.*

South Florida from '82 to '87 was a high flyin' time. Of course we didn't have much money so it was the budget version. After living in a one-room closet for a year, I moved into an old converted horse stall we called the "Shack." The only vegetation was a couple weeds in the dirt. My brother came down to stay for a few years. We battled roof rats and were visited by a family of Jehovah's Witnesses who brought along their very attractive daughter. She made a good pitch, but I wasn't ready to catch anything. Besides there already was another girl intent on guiding my spiritual awakening.

Sometime in the winter of '84 I met John "The Worm" Laprey, and he had a healthy thirst for life even if it meant having to feed the frogs the next morning. John got me to feel more comfortable about playing my guitar in front of people at barbecues and the like.

He always seemed to have roommates who were on their way to insanity or premature death. One of them was once on a weekend drunk and threatening to kill his boss or somebody so John took his shotgun and wanted to leave it at my place until the guy either passed out or calmed down. He was nothing compared to the guy who literally slept with his dog, but that's another man's story.

The old lady who owned the shack eventually went senile and started accusing me of stealing furniture and not believing in God. She watched those preachers on television all day long and her thinking was wound-up pretty tight by that point so my brother and I moved out that fall.

We ended up living in this whitewashed apartment next to the railroad tracks. The landlord was a middle man in the coke trade, yet there were some nice old folks and young people living there. A lot of cockroaches too so we'd collect lizards and let them live with us.

I met a lot of crazy people during the next few years. Gypsy-types who were only passing through or there for the winter. One of them was this guy we called Montana Tom who lived on the Blackfoot Indian Reservation in Montana which was only possible due to his having married a Blackfoot girl who subsequently was killed in a car accident. Tom was only in south

Florida long enough to make it with seven girls, alienate a lot of our simple working folk crowd with his tales of endless travel and enterprise (he bought and sold clothes and jewelry from central America and did some harvesting work between time), and show me the magical tones and textures of mandolin playing. He learned half a dozen of my songs, including "Lovin' The Alien" and promised to spread the word by singing them out west. According to people who've visited him there, he's kept his word.

Poisoned Wheat

*Last night I dreamed of a sky painted blue
And a place I remember
Where all my dreams came true,
And when I awoke
And looked into the sky,
I knew what I saw,
But I did not know why.*

*You ever get that feeling
That something aint right.
You know it's really daytime,
But you cannot see the light.
Hunger don't mean nothin'
If there's nothin' to eat.
It's like standing in a field
That's full of poisoned wheat.*

*My father used to tell me,
"Take only what you need.
You can't pick the cotton, boy,
Until you've laid the seed.
Don't take nothin', son,
You know you can't return,
And you'll never teach a man
what he don't want to learn.*

*Yes, and hunger don't mean nothin'
If there's nothin' to eat.
It's like standing in a field
That's full of poisoned wheat."*

*I remember Daddy's words
As I sit up tonight
Waiting for a stranger
To come turn off the light.
Tell me, dear sweet God,
If I kneel down to pray,
Why did tomorrow
Just arrive today?*

*You ever get that feeling
That something aint right?
You know it's really daytime,
But it looks just like last night.
Hunger don't mean nothin'
If there's nothin' to eat.
It's like standing in a field
That's full of poisoned wheat.*

Justice Prevails

Black man hangin' from a willow tree
In the moonlight where wild rivers run free.
Another man digging himself a ditch
'cause he got caught trying to get rich.

And here's to the land of liberty,
And here's to the end of slavery,
And here's to the ghettoes, the projects and the jails
And here's to a country where justice prevails

They used to ride horses on the plains
'till the men with the fire and brimstone came.
They took the land, the air, and sea.
Killin' in the name of God for greed.

And here's to the glory of the past,
And here's to the final, silent blast,
Here's to the buffalo, the wolf and the whales
And here's to a world where justice prevails

Little girl lost out on the street
Lookin' for something she can eat,
While the President rides his silver horse,
And the sun is shining on the green golf course.

And here's to the sick and the poor,
Here's to the widows of the war,
Yes, and here's to the Harvards, the Princetons and the Yales
And here's to the future where justice prevails

*If you told me all my eyes have seen
Was nothing more than a crazy dream,
I'd ask ya how could ya compromise,
Spit at truth, and believe in lies?*

*Yes, and here's to the loss of memory,
And here's to the dead young men set free,
And here's to the hero, the one who never fails
As he cries out in the darkness, "Justice prevails."*

Distant Galaxy

They say one man's misfortune
Is another man's good luck.
I tried to reach you last evening,
But I've been out of touch.
It's hard for me to believe
That I'm not as young as I used to be,
Yesterday's so far away
Like a distant galaxy.

I remember how you used to sing,
You were never quite in key,
But I never felt that beauty
Had to be a perfect harmony.
There was something in the way you moved
From one man to the next,
Always giving each all your love
'till there was nothing left.

I feel like I'm a carpenter
Who's come from Galilee
With so much left to give you
Still you turn away from me.
Summer's rose is fading
As the chill of fall moves on.
Time to take what I have gained,
Say good-bye to what is gone.

From Dog Beach to Crescent Street: 1985-1988

1985 was an oddly intoxicating time. I took this big trip out west just to see the place and suck it in. Mountains and rivers and fat retired people in monstrous motor homes. I read Bury My Heart At Wounded Knee *that year and found myself amazed at my own ignorance. Alone and silent I drove on through deserts and thunderstorms. I think Live Aid was happening at this time. Meanwhile I saw my first buffalo and, perhaps I was dreaming, heard a coyote cry.*

Did the traveling help my writing? It must have later on as everything experienced does to some extent. But I wrote most of the decent lyrics ("Thousand Miles of Land" and "There's Always Some Place") before I took off. Who was it that said the best cowboy songs were written by Jewish city boys living in New York? There's some truth to that I suppose.

There's Always Some Place

Angelina was a-dreamin'
Of a lover she let get away,
While Joseph was a-cussin'
'bout the gov'ment
And the bills he couldn't pay,

And the children were listening
To the songs on their one radio,
Yes, and there's always some place
Better than the one that you know.

One night in the springtime
Angelina put on her old coat,
Joseph was off drinking,
He didn't know that
She'd started to smoke,

And the children were listening
To the songs on their one radio,
Yes, and there's always some place
Better than the one that you know.

Angelina's got a lover
Who's got nothin'
'cept something that she needs,
And Joseph's always angry,
And he hates everything that he sees.

Angelina was a-dreamin'
Of some place she'd always wanted to go,
And the children were still listening
To the songs on their one radio.

A Thousand Miles of Land

*Tomorrow I'm a-headed
To Eldorado, Texas,
I got a job
Workin' for some man,
Says he owns
A thousand miles of land.*

*Give my love to Katy,
She's my favorite lady,
But she needs
Another kind of man,
The kind who owns
A thousand miles of land.*

*I don't mind digging ditches,
Beats cleaning dirty dishes,
I'm getting tired
Of being where I am,
Hell, I never even seen
A thousand miles of land.*

*I'm goin' west to make some bread,
All I see's blue skies ahead,
Better days just around the bend.
Paid some dues and all my debts,
Leaving here with no regrets,
Don't know if I'll be this way again.*

Life is what you make it,
I don't think I could take it
So I'm gonna deal myself
A better hand,
There's new life yonder
On a thousand miles of land.

Forever I'll Be True

"George, George, George,
The ceiling's falling down,
There's water in the basement,
And I ripped my wedding gown.
I tell you, George,
We're getting married none too soon,
Please come save me
And forever I'll be true."

"George, George, George,
The baby's on the way,
I think I'm in labor now,
And the bills need to be paid.
The insurance company called,
They say we're overdue.
Please come save me
And forever I'll be true."

"George, George, George,
Where were you late last night?
I waited up 'till midnight
And left on the kitchen light.
I tell you, George,
Little Danny's got a cold,
The bank wants back its money
And at twenty I feel old."

"George, George, George,
Am I asking for too much?
Sometimes you get so distant,
And I feel so out of touch.
There's nothing in the world
That I wouldn't do,
Please come save me
And forever I'll be true."

"George, George, George,
Are you gone for good?
I've tried so hard to make it work,
I've done everything I could.
I tell you, George,
It's true that I love you,
Please come save me
And forever I'll be true."

"George, George, George,
Why'd you go and run away,
Leave me with three children
And these bills I cannot pay?
I hope you finish up
Whatever you've got to do,
Then please come save me
And forever I'll be true."

Long As You Know

I was driving down the road on a hot summer night,
I was feeling kind of low, but hey that's all right,
Long as you know you've got some other place to go.

Well, there's war and there's more war everywhere you look,
You can see it on TV or you can read it in a book,
Long as you know you've got some other place to go.

Now they advertise for gold unholy love,
And they talk about His kingdom from high above,
Long as you know you've got some other place to go.

My god's in the earth, the river, and the wind,
My god aint a king, my god she's my friend,
Long as you know you've got some other place to go.

Now even if the trouble's been there all your life,
Pain takes no vacation, and misery's your wife,
Long as you know you've got some other place to go.

So here I am again on a Saturday night,
Lost out on the highway, looking for the light,
Long as you know you've got some other place to go.

Lovin' The Alien

*My thoughts they may be noble
In a darker age,
But in this enlightened one
They put me in a cage.
I got thrown in jail
For makin' love to a girl.
How was I to know
She was from some other world?*

*I don't care if she's got green skin,
Just wanna be lovin' the alien.
Who knows where that unit's been?
Just wanna be lovin' the alien.
Outer space has got lots of room,
And love's hard to find beyond the moon,
If God forgives a man's worst sin,
Why can't I be lovin' the alien?*

*Now on the subject of marriage.
My daddy always said
If she was black he'd kill,
Mom prayed a lot,
Said she'd likely get ill.
Now time heals all wounds,
Too bad it can't heal hate.
My alien friend says she can't relate.*

*I don't care if she's got green skin,
Just wanna be lovin' the alien.
Who knows where that unit's been?
Just wanna be lovin' the alien.
Outer space has got lots of room,
And love's hard to find beyond the moon,
If God forgives a man's worst sin,
Why can't I be lovin' the alien?*

*Now my girlfriend's cold,
She's got to make heat,
She needs to borrow
Both of my feet.*

*Her death will lie
Upon your soul,
And space is such a
Deep, dark hole.*

*People been persecuted
Throughout all of time,
And the history books
Are filled with crime,
Greed and violence,
Death and fear,
My girlfriend wants to know
What I'm still doing here.
That's a good question
Coming from an alien.*

*Yeah, I don't care if she's got green skin,
Just wanna be lovin' the alien.
Who knows where that unit's been?
Just wanna be lovin' the alien.
Outer space has got lots of room,
And love's hard to find beyond the moon,
If God forgives a man's worst sin,
Why can't I be lovin' the alien?*

*Now it's time for me
To make my escape,
Remember me
When you hear this tape
As just a kid
Who had to follow his heart
And is up there somewhere
In the light of them stars.*

Touch of Her Smile

Off in the distance somebody's getting married.
Bless these people, their house, and their child,
And don't forget after a thousand mornings after,
You still remember the touch of her smile.

And she's somewhere I don't know maybe out at sea,
Maybe she's living in the distance or the
    woods of the old country,
Maybe she's found her fortune in the birth of a second chance,
Maybe she works all day making the old broom dance.

But I know that she smiles
Why and with whom well oh well
I know that she smiles
I can tell.

The bells are ringing like some siren out of reach,
And the wind keeps blowing her memories back at me.
The virgins look so vacant like an empty parking lot,
And the whores look like they get screwed
    a lot more than a lot.

Yes, and I know that she smiles
Why and with whom well oh well
I know that she smiles
I can tell.

The train's heading out to a place I once called home.
I know the feeling of the man who sails alone.
Sometimes I hear her like a silent screaming light
That wakes me up to face the darkness of the night.

*I know that she smiles
Why and with whom well oh well
I know that she smiles
I can tell.*

*Off in the distance somebody's getting married.
Bless these people, their house, and their child,
And don't forget after a thousand mornings after,
You still remember the touch of her smile.*

I'll never forget the day I left Florida for what I thought would be the last time. It was early June of '87. I had packed up all my belongings, mostly records and two beat-up suitcases filled with writings and old newspaper clippings. My used vehicle at this time was a third-hand Ford econoline van. I took a swing in it down to Dog Beach to pick up Teresa who needed a ride to St. Augustine. Must have been mid-morning — I walked down to the bench that looked out on the ocean. MaryAnn sat there. She looked like a young Mary Travers. We both watched the ocean for awhile. It was choppy and bright yellow from the sun. That warm briny breeze was trying to tell me something, but my thoughts were elsewhere. MaryAnn was still sore about the way I had treated one of her girlfriends, but the day was too spectacular for anybody to hold a grudge too long.

This was the end of a piece of time, and at that moment I wasn't in the mood to look back. We sat thirty yards from John's apartment at the Pelican. It was there just before leaving Florida that I wrote "Touch of Her Smile" and where I met an odd assortment of surfers and drifters mixed in with some redneck natives and assorted oddballs. This guy Danny and his old lady Dawn lived next door to John. He had a pet rattlesnake and shot squirrels from his porch. He was damn good lookin', a fine dancer, and admitted to liking the B-52's. I put him in my song about Florida, "Mister Meger's Store." He's a carpenter, and he and Dawn had a couple of kids before he one day just disappeared.

When I got on the road, Teresa wanted to know what I had planned. To tell the truth I had no idea, but I felt something was stirring inside me, and I was eager to write without interruption. I was leaving the comfort of some decent guitar players who supported me, John and Paul Hitchon. I knew that certain songs like "Justice Prevails" and "Runaway" only needed the proper musical context. They were good songs. But I didn't head straight to some place like Greenwich Village. After a stop in St. Louis, I gunned it for the place of my youth, Westerly, Rhode Island.

*"Underneath that tree
There's just gonna be you and me
Underneath that old
apple suckling tree"*

—*Bob Dylan*

Certain situations and circumstances in life must have been meant to happen. From June, 1987 to December, 1988 was when I stumbled upon such a moment. I drove back to New England in the rain. Pulled in one Sunday night and went straight to the Knickerbocker Cafe to see if Roomful of Blues was still playing there. Of course they weren't, and I stood there in the bleak drizzle having arrived home to an empty greeting.

As always my grandma came to the rescue and let me move in for awhile. I got a job spray painting guitars in the Guild factory and kept writing lyrics. My old buddy Fred Buffum came down on weekends, and we played a lot that fall. I watched autumn for the first time in six years, and I kept writing.

Sometime in February I started collaborating with Joel O'Lari who had an eight track recording studio set up in this garage on the golf course. We drank a bit of beer and somehow Joel got me to loosen up enough to actually sing these songs into his machine. He then spent months producing a musical atmosphere for them, and I must say nobody I've ever played with has come as close to matching his guitar licks to the meaning of the lyrics.

It was during this time that I wrote the bulk of lyrics that still stick out in my mind as the best I can do. Alone in Gran's basement I wrote "Invisible Man," "Basement Blues," and "Red Sox Fan." Come summertime I was living at Joel's place on Crescent Street where one afternoon I penned "Cooper's Farewell" which was bits and pieces of actual facts capped off with a fictional ending. I ended up marrying the girl, but before I did I wrote all these songs. Working in a guitar factory gave me plenty of time to think for myself so that's what I did.

The Return of Old Sparky

In a twelve by nineteen room
Made out of concrete block
There sits an old oak chair
That used to get real hot.
It's been a long time
Since they fed it some juice,
This once humane advancement
That one day replaced the noose.

They say Old Sparky's
Gonna burn again,
Gonna fry the bad guys,
Save all that money
We don't want to spend.
There's only one problem
They've got to work out first,
Nobody remembers
How the damn thing works.

They've got these half-windows
Where witnesses can watch
One of the bad guys
Get zapped right on the spot.
Now they call it justice,
Return of the iron fist
After all those wishy-washy years
When we just slapped 'em on the wrist.

*Hey, hey Old Sparky's
Gonna burn again,
Gonna broil the bad guys,
Aint that a powerful
Message to send?
There's only one problem
They've got to work out first,
How in the hell
Do we get this thing to work?*

*The last man to get it
In this New England state
Was a man they called Mad Dog
Who in 1960 met his fate.
Now they've got this Michael Ross
Who will soon be put to death.
Another day he might have gotten away
Or had a rope around his neck.*

*Now they've got Old Sparky
Who's got a job again,,
Gonna fry the bad guys,
Bring their killing days to an end.
There's only one problem
When they figure out how it works,
Another killing's been done.
Who's to say which one is worse?*

Mr. Meger's Store

*Mr. Wilson Megers was the owner
Of a little country store in Florida.
He sold cold beer, bait and soda,
And had a wife who he never loved.
His two girls were both fat and friendly,
They used to sweat a lot and like to laugh,
And on those days when it was hot as a hog's breath,
The sisters went out back to take a bath.*

*And if you're a tourist from up north you might think that
This wasn't a very pleasant way to live,
But just think for a moment before you pass judgment,
Most people just do the best with what they get.*

*Nancy Curtin is a widow,
Her husband got shot and killed in the war.
She never bothered to get remarried,
But she got a job in Mr. Meger's store.
She doesn't talk much to the sisters,
She listens and chain smokes Lucky Strikes.
On Sundays sometimes she goes fishing,
And she always watches Magnum on Wednesday nights.*

*And if you're a tourist from up north you might think that
This wasn't a very pleasant way to live,
But just think for a moment before you pass judgment,
Most people just do the best with what they get.*

Danny boy is proud to be a native,
He shoots squirrels and skins 'em on his porch.
When it comes to Yanks he'd rather be with the gators,
He don't like the blue noses from up North.
His sister Linda had an operation
So he went to visit her every day.
Then he'd come home and put on Hank Williams Jr.
And listen to that wildass kick and play.

On Sunday Danny was going fishing
So he stopped off at Mr. Meger's store
Where Nancy was listening to the sisters
Who were talking about some dress Joan Collins wore.
Nancy handed Danny his chew of tobacco
And told him to get his own bait out back.
Meanwhile the sisters kept on sweating,
Now they were talking about Blake Carrington's Cadillac.

And if you're a tourist from up north you might think that
This wasn't a very pleasant way to live,
But just think for a moment before you pass judgment,
Most people just do the best with what they get.

Ballad of the Boston Red Sox Fan (1986-1987)

Well the Boston Red Sox are my favorite team,
I been rooting for them since the Impossible Dream,
Yeah, remember Yastrzemski and the great George Scott,
And Jimmy Lonborg when he was really hot,
A pennant and the triple crown
But oh that seventh game,
It was in the Cards and Bob Gibson reigned.

I'm a Red Sox Fan.

For a while I got too tired to even give a damn,
I even traded in my cap and retired as a fan,
But lo and behold they went wild in '75,
Fisk hit that home run that kept the team alive,
But Cincinnati won that awful seventh game,
And somehow I aint ever quite been the same.

I'm a Red Sox Fan.

Now the Red Sox have always gotten plenty of hits,
But Fenway's a hellova place to have to pitch,
However that all changed in 1986
When an age old problem had finally been fixed.

Remember our pitchers like the famed Ray Culp,
With him on the mound the game was rarely dull,
And Bill "Spaceman" Lee smokin' dope after games,
And all those great pitchers we traded away
like Sparki Lyle and some guy they called the Babe.

Yeah, we've sure had a lot of lemons,
But now we've got Roger Clemens,
And I'm a Red Sox Fan.

We might be cynical and say they'll somehow lose again,
But we always cheer 'em on, love and hate 'em like a friend,
They're in our hearts and our souls way deep,
And still you might say I've lost a lot of sleep.

I'm a Red Sox Fan.

Now we said, "Look homeward, Angels,
   come on Mighty Mets.
We've been the underdog all year, had
   to come back from death,
Just ask Dave Henderson about missing that catch,
He'll be proud to show you his home run bat.
Yeah, we might never quite lose the past,
But right now we've got a World Series to crash.

And I'm a Red Sox Fan."

And there we were in game number six,
All we needed was one more good pitch,
It was already decided Bruce Hurst was MVP,
But you know what they say,
"Some things just weren't meant to be.

I'm a Red Sox Fan."

*So stand up and cheer the courage of Bill,
Remember the games with those late inning thrills,
Sing praise to Dewey in right all them years,
And Mr. Jim Rice who's heard the boos and the cheers,
Here's to Rico and Luis, the great El T,
Reggie and Billy, the Hawk and Tony C.,
And to Number 8 and to number 9,
Johnny Pesky and all those guys before my time,
Somewhere they're all watching the game today,
And deep in their hearts you can hear them say,*

*"I'm a Red Sox Fan,
Come on, Oil Can."*

Goin' To The Record Store

I woke up early on a Saturday morning,
Had the whole world in my hands.
You see I just got paid the day before
So I stuffed a couple tens in my pants.
No need for a comb I just grabbed my hat
And had myself a shot of OJ,
Got my bicycle out of the garage,
Left a note on the door,
The one I leave on every day.

"Hey Ma, I'll see you later,
When I get back I'll do all my chores,
But right now I got me a date with heaven,
I'm goin' to the record store."

Goin' to the record, goin' to the record,
Goin' to the record store.

It doesn't matter if it's in the springtime,
The fall or the summer or the wintertime.
It's just that when it's snowin' and sleetin' outside,
Well, it's kinda hard to ride my bike.
My friends all call me a music junkie,
My teachers say I'm wastin' my time,
But I would just like to remind all concerned parties
Whatever time I've got is mine.

"Hey Ma, I'll see you later,
When I'm older I will give all my money to the poor,
But right now I got me a date with heaven,
I'm goin' to the record store."

Goin' to the record, goin' to the record,
Goin' to the record store.

I've spent the night in line for concert tickets,
I've traveled days just to see the band.
Yeah, youth is strange and I've done some things
My parents might not understand,
But my folks are pretty cool,
They have faith in me
That I will treat my freedom like a friend.
My dad says to have a good time, son,
I might not get the chance again.

"Hey Ma, I'll see you later,
When I get home I'll fix the screen door,
But right now I got me a date with heaven,
I'm goin' to the record store."

Goin' to the record, goin' to the record,
Goin' to the record store.

Invisible Man

When you're feelin' like a stranger in your own hometown,
And nobody you used to know is ever around,
The beer still tastes good but not like it once did
On those hot summer nights when you were still a kid.

Yes, I am an invisible man
I'm not black but I do understand
What it's like not to be seen as I am,
An invisible man, an invisible man

I've got dreams I've kept secret and desire in mind,
I've been given a number and told to stand in line,
I see people lookin' at me like I'm up on the wall,
It gets so I don't think they see me at all.

Yes, I am an invisible man
I'm not black but I do understand
What it's like not to be seen as I am,
An invisible man, an invisible man

Well, the water is still but my reflection's disappeared,
There's no me in the mirror I guess I'm no longer here,
All it takes is one night one voice to touch,
But maybe I'm askin' for a little too much.

Yes, I am an invisible man
I'm not black but I do understand
What it's like not to be seen as I am,
An invisible man, an invisible man

Basement Blues

When you're as high as the night is long as the darkest road,
And you've got no one you can talk to so your secret's untold,
And there's all sorts of boxes of things that you've kept
Like so much dust that never got swept.

All I ever wanted was a love like I had with you,
But there aint no light tonight just these basement blues,
Oh, the basement blues, yeah, the basement blues.

When you're riding the train into the city by the sea,
Do your thoughts drift back to that
    time when you wanted me?
Did you keep my picture or did you just throw it away?
I've still got the one of you I just brushed it off yesterday.

All I ever wanted was a love like I had with you,
But there aint no light tonight just these basement blues,
Oh, the basement blues, yeah, the basement blues.

When you're feeling like the healing
    aint happening fast enough,
And even your doctor tells you to stay off of love,
And God how you wish you could be back in the rain
Singing like an ocean in your chains.

All I ever wanted was a love like I had with you,
But there aint no light tonight just these basement blues,
Oh, the basement blues, yeah, the basement blues.

Positively Bobby

There's a dog down my street tonight,
In the dark he calls my name.
I'm feelin' cold as a bag of bones,
I wish the weather would change.

I thought I heard you say you'd be faithful,
Then I saw the writing on the wall.
I could tell that the ink was still wet,
Said something about anytime being a good time to call.

And now I'm Positively Bobby
There's a poison in my veins
My heart feels like a dartboard
My blood is cold as rain

You didn't think I'd notice the lipstick
My best friend had on his sleeve?
Who were you trying to hurt more anyway?
Was it him or was it me?

Yeah, I'm feelin' pretty apocalyptic
Like I'm a witness to the Fall,
But when I'm standing outside your window
I don't feel nothin' really at all.

And now I'm Positively Bobby
There's a poison in my veins
My heart feels like a dartboard
My blood is cold as rain

You don't believe me do you well now
Why would I lie like that?
Once upon a time you even trusted me.
Did I really treat you so bad?

I never did expect you to be the kind
Who would always stick around.
Especially when I saw your eyes light up
When the circus came to town.

And now I'm Positively Bobby
There's a poison in my veins
My heart feels like a dartboard
My blood is cold as rain

You said it had nothing to do with me,
It was something inside of you.
You said I couldn't fulfill all your needs,
Kinda funny after all we've been through.

Remember goin' down to the beach,
February in the moonlight,
I can't believe there's anything better in the world
Than the way we made love that night.

Now I wear my armor like a badge
But truthfully it doesn't work,
Whenever I hear somebody laughing out there,
I remember where it hurts.

*And now I'm Positively Bobby
There's a poison in my veins
My heart feels like a dartboard
My blood is cold as rain*

Eight months in a guitar factory, nobody who worked there ever knew I had been a teacher, prep, college graduate. I punched in my card every morning and did my job. Met some "real nice" people there and a couple of punks. This one kid, Tim, we got along great, but he was wired. He told me about how he fell asleep in a friend's car, and some other guy stole the car and flipped it. Tim was thrown out and only bruised but the guy was pinned in the car, gas was everywhere, and it was anyone's guess when or if the car would blow. The guy begged for help, but Tim just stood there cussing him out and saying he was psyched to watch the thieving motherf-er burn. The cops rescued the guy, but Tim never moved. Another guy there was a choir-singing, devout Catholic who happened to be gay and assumed his guilt and said he'd go to hell but he was a believer in God's mercy despite people's judgment of him. He was a kind old toothless guy shaped like a bowling pin. Said he used to hang out in the park and service hard-up boys. His tales added a weird dimension to my view of this quaint little middle-class town.

While spray-painting guitars and writing nightly in Gran's basement, I eventually got the hankering to start up some friendships. My brother had landed a new painting job, and he was living in Stonington having abandoned the comfort of his old VW bus. So he'd keep in touch, but more and more I found myself visiting Joel, his roomie Spence, and Val at Crescent Street, a place Spence described as "a haven for all the stray cats and mutts of Westerly." Not used to the winter winds, I found comfort and warmth there despite their lack of funds to keep the thermostat at a decent temp. It was there I met this profoundly disturbed young woman who was in the midst of a divorce despite her strict religious upbringing. She was rather conflicted, so I tried to ease her guilt by ranting about the treatment of the ghost dancing Sioux at the hands of good, Christian soldiers who slaughtered women and children and compared to that, I assured her, divorce was a forgivable sin. I don't I believe I assuaged her feelings of failure, her faith in God trumping my rationalizations. But as Randle P. McMurphy said, "At least I tried, damnit, at least I did that much."

Crescent Street, meanwhile, provided me with an outlet for my twisted imagination and unorthodox world view. By February, Joel and I were recording a couple times a week down at the garage. Other nights I'd stop by the apartment just to hang out. There was some real crust to the place, but the people were genuine, intelligent, free spirits as much as working people who accept the fact a man's got to work can be. Joel had the talent to head off and be discovered in some city, but he didn't have the temperament or desire to quit a world he felt comfortable in. Instead he builtt a home studio and jammed with local boys, which was my good fortune.

Watching The Dark Rain

When you can't trust the soap that's in your hands,
And you can't trust the water in your drain,
And you don't know what kind of pill it is
They just told you to take for the pain,
And you keep hearin' the drillin' in the walls,
And the screamin' in your head never goes away,
Won't you come see me, Mary Jane.

When you reach out to touch and nobody is there,
And you think maybe your judgment can't be repaired,
And the damage of life just makes you scared,
And by tomorrow you could be left unaware,
Won't you come see me, Mary Jane.

Yes, we'll watch the dark rain
Like we did yesterday,
And we'll drink in the silence,
And need nothing to say,
Watching the dark rain
Watching the dark rain
Watching the dark rain

When you wish a decision could be settled and made,
And you want everything wrapped up
   'cause it's easy that way,
And you know the card's marked, but
   the hand must be played,
And while you can speak say what you've got to say,
And you can always come see me, Mary Jane,
And we'll both sit there and watch
The dark rain.

Guild Factory Blues

*It sucks when you have to work all day
In a factory where you make little pay,
And then the government and union come
To take all your money away,
But you've got a job so what can you say?*

*Every morning at seven o'clock
I punch in my card and place it in the same spot.
It's either too friggin' cold or else it's too damn hot,
And there's a hundred good reasons
    why some men drink a lot.*

*They started me out stickin' on pick guards.
Now they've got me spray paintin' their guitars.
Maybe one of them I spray will be played
By one of them big, old rock 'n' roll stars.
Hey, it's something to talk about Friday in the bars.*

*Every morning all I see's eight hours ahead.
I could be in some better place but I'm here instead.
I know this factory keeps a lot of these families fed,
And maybe there's nothing more need be said.*

*I know for me there's got to be a better way.
Tomorrow's got to be a promise not the same as yesterday.
A lot of these people have no choice but to stay,
And they've got a job so what can they say?*

Find Your Love

Tera, my friend,
Do you believe in reincarnation?
Did I know you before?
I hope I get to know you again.
The landscape is quite smoky,
And love is hard to find.
I hope that you
Find your love in time.

Frustration is rampant;
Disillusion barkin' everywhere.
You know that I'd be lyin'
If I told you that I didn't care.
Tera, my friend,
Love is hard to find.
I hope that you
Find your love in time.

How can you be so casual?
Your eyes they always smile.
Now that I'm supposed to be a man,
How come I feel just like a child?

Tera, my friend,
Do you believe in a drifting soul?
Are you an old friend
Or am I imagining
Something I can't hold?
Tera, my friend,
Love is hard to find.
I hope that you
Find your love in time.

In The Springtime

I was not born out of sorrow,
I was not born out of fear,
Just two people makin' love one night,
And that is why I am here.

They made love in the springtime,
Must have been sometime in May,
For all the trouble and the heartache,
Sometimes things just go your way.

There's a mighty ragin' river
Rollin' out to the sea,
Sometimes the wind does deliver,
And faith is always good company.

And I've made love in the springtime,
Before I knew just what to say,
For all the trouble and the heartache,
Sometimes things just go your way.

But I've seen too much anger,
Hatred only brings you down,
It's always money and government,
They sure do twist good folk around.

I was not born to be a rich man,
Nor was I born to be poor,
I was born in a hospital
Just after the war.

They made love in the springtime,
Must have been sometime in May,
For all the trouble and the heartache,
Sometimes things just go your way.

Cooper's Farewell

I knew a sad little woman who moaned too often
'cause she don't know what to do.
Her daughter grew up completely corrupted,
Kinda reminds me of you.
And you don't know what I been through
All the mornings after I last saw you.
The bridge was crossed, the river roared,
The king and his men all looking bored,
When was the last time we had a war?

I knew a man who was often confused
By the politics of love.
He used to consume barrels of rum
And laugh at the man above.
You don't know what I been through,
Even I don't always want solitude.
The road was closed, the rain was late,
Are we supposed to sit here and wait?
Who among you cares to relate?

Innocence was slaughtered and photographed
When you and I were young.
We both stood and watched the awful scene,
Part of who we were among.
Ah, but you don't know what I been through,
And I've forgotten the good I knew.
Still the spring is like it once was,
Why's that, Dad? Well, just because
Dreams are born and they do get busted.

*My sister was into this woman who wrote
Like her life was an open book.
She knew every word was absolutely true.
Imagine the pain that took.
You don't know what I been through,
And I don't know the same about you.
The dawn is dark, the silence cold,
The life you live is bought and sold,
And I'm still trying to find my way back home.*

*I've watched her smoke and sigh out loud,
Well-versed in what she feels,
While the boys are in the canteen store
Before they ride their wheels.
"And you don't know what I been through,"
She said to me as I rode away too.
"The door is open, it's still unlocked,
You don't even have to knock,
But if you go now,
Don't ever stop."*

*I rode away, I rode away
I rode away, I rode away*

Grandma Told Me So

In the kingdom of the lion,
The mother goes to hunt.
She's known to do whatever it takes
When it's time to feed her young.
She's got a certain dignity
In her pride and in her life.
Grandma told me so last night.

In the years of the Depression,
Many families had no work.
People did whatever it took;
A lot of folk got hurt.
But you've got to keep the faith
That things will turn out right.
Grandma told me so last night.

She told me 'bout the years of rain
And that big, old hurricane,
How the houses were swept away
Only to be built again,
How fate is so funny,
And how it's sad to witness change.

In the realms of nature's mystery,
Many secret lives will thrive;
But if man remains so careless,
Nothing will survive.
What you do or don't do
Will affect the planet's life.
Grandma told me so last night.

She told me 'bout the garden
Her family grew in time of war.
She told me 'bout the good years
And the fancy clothes she wore,
And how she misses
Those times more and more.

The stars are very useful;
They can tell us many things;
But you may never know
The fortune fate may bring.
Go carve your own path,
And in the end you'll see the light.
Grandma told me so last night.

Summer of '88 I moved into Crescent Street to further continue the collaboration with Joel. He did enlist the help of Eastcoast Johnny who played some harp and slide dobro on "Mr. Megar's Store" and a few others. We spent a lot of time doing double-up vocal tracks to help boost the performances already recorded on the eight track. Joel put an awful lot of time and energy into the "Acoustic" project, and I am in debt to him to this day.

One summer afternoon I found myself thinking about all the different women in my past and present and how it seemed like I was always driving away from one of them. I wrote "Cooper's Farewell" in one afternoon. Words didn't fail me and I immediately put it to music without even stopping to think about it. Joel got me to record the song while it was still fresh. I have a hard time remembering all of the different choruses to this song except when I feel the need to sing it.

When I pulled out of Westerly that August, Joel even went so far as to step outside for a proper send-off. It had been only seven months since our first recording session, and yet it had been a lifetime's experience. Creating art is the greatest high imaginable. What were once just words of mine had become part of a living, breathing art form — music. And despite my obvious limitations, Joel had insisted we build the songs around my rhythm guitar and that I sing the songs. We did take after take until my untrained warbling at least didn't fail because of lack of passion. "Let's nail it this time," he would say, and I've never quit trying ever since this odd reclusive guitar genius showed me some patience and faith.

So I headed for St. Louis to see my mom before the trip south. I was returning to my old teaching job and a world I thought I left for good, but that's my life for you. I never know quite what's going to happen next, and that doesn't bother me.

"Where are you, Walt?
The open road goes to the used car lot."
—*Louis Simpson*

Woodbox and Harp: 1989-1992

When I returned to Florida I was pretty much experiencing writer burn-out, though I didn't want to admit it. I had confronted myself in song and somehow came out of it ready to get married and settle into something closer to safety, lifestyle-wise. I drove back south proud of what I'd done but unaware of how much I would miss Joel and those days. Wherever I go I'm always romanticizing about the place I've just been or the next place I'm headed.

At the time John was still in Florida, so for three months we played guitars every day after work. Once while we were playing, a neighbor called the police because he was afraid someone was being strangled. Actually John was just trying to sing like Neil Young and he couldn't quite hit all those notes.

Vick and I moved into this great house with an upstairs floor made of cypress. We called it the studio, and made it our rejuvenation center. The landlord was this woman who later went to jail for involvement in the cocaine trade. That type was still around. Great place to spend a year, but we eventually had to move. While there I did write "Tropical Moonshine" and "Phil Spector's Blues," the former eventually becoming one of Joel's signature songs which he recorded on Green Tea's second CD. Meanwhile, I kept my hand at writing lyrics, but it never amounted to much. I played a lot of music, but I had nothing new to say for the next two and a half years.

Tropical Moonshine

*Cold pink clouds and that wind of steel,
My nose is runnin', Lord knows how I feel.
I don't mind walkin' that empty street,
It's just that now even my dreams are bleak.*

*I need a dose of tropical moonshine
I need the hope that I lost in the meantime
Won't you take me down that southbound freight line
Where the air is nice
In plastic paradise
Tropical moonshine
Tropical moonshine*

*The elephant man saw the zebra girl,
And it was love at first sight in the animal world.
The future aint people afraid of themselves,
Say good-bye to those who don't wish you well.*

*I need a dose of tropical moonshine
I need the hope that I lost in the meantime
Won't you take me down that southbound freight line
Where the air is nice
In plastic paradise
Tropical moonshine
Tropical moonshine*

The Negro shacks in snow look soft,
While chimneys burn and children cough.
It's so hard to believe
That lovers laugh in such poverty.

I need a dose of tropical moonshine
I need the hope that I lost in the meantime
Won't you take me down that southbound freight line
Where the air is nice
In plastic paradise
Tropical moonshine
Tropical moonshine

I Came For You

It must have been something I said in
    a letter I wrote long ago
When my words were like wind and I was paper thin
Holdin' onto her breast in the cold.

The battles of passion like weather stretch
    your skin 'till you're old,
'till all you've got left is half-forgotten at best,
And even the seeds that you sow don't take hold.

I came for you, I came for you
After all the mad scenes and the dreams
    that we've been through
I came for you, I came for you

Too many people in the kitchen bitchin'
    'bout their petty lives,
There's a fork in the road my spoon-fed child,
You could cut meat with those eyes.

Ah, she decided to go back to Houston,
    you thought it a big mistake.
You gotta know when to call it useless and
    pack up that old heartache.

I came for you, I came for you
After all the mad scenes and the dreams
    that we've been through
I came for you, I came for you

*The dawn was on the horizon, unaware of God's intent
While your brother counted up his earnings
And spent his dope money on the rent.*

*The jukebox in the slaughterhouse played my favorite song,
You got confused when I lost the fuse
But still you had the sense to hang on.*

*I came for you, I came for you
After all the mad scenes and the dreams
    that we've been through
I came for you, I came for you*

*Maybe Sam Shepard was right when he
    shot his foot with the truth,
You can't go back to Freeport now,
But we still might find Duluth.*

*I came for you, I came for you
After all the mad scenes and the dreams
    that we've been through
I came for you, I came for you*

Phil Spector's Blues

*When you can't feel the lovin' anymore
And you're dyin' to get outside these emotional wars;
One minute you're numb, the next you're full of rage,
And you can't pull the trigger or turn the page.*

*Won't you come surfin' with me?
I never done it before but in my mind I know I can see
An endless summer-like sunset
And dreams of a southern breeze.
Won't you come surfin' with me?*

*Hey, Brian Wilson is still alive;
You know he faced the darkness down inside,
Alone in the morning close to those ocean waves,
Uncertain tomorrow would be like yesterday.*

*Won't you come surfin' with me?
We can ride on the wind absolutely free.
I could be laughed at or passed off so easily
Or have nobody out there recognize me.
Won't you come surfin' with me?*

*Functional but static we become
Not even close to what we thought when we were young,
And for a moment you used to believe in a feelin'
You aint been receivin' and now that it's evening.*

*Won't you come surfin' with me?
I never done it before but in my mind I know I can see
An endless summer-like sunset
And dreams of a southern breeze.
Won't you come surfin' with me?*

Some Other Place

I was hurt and angry when I was just a child
At the thought of separation and her painful goodbye smile.
I dried the tears inside me and showed my bravest face,
Swallowed hard the words I heard,
She gone some other place.

When I was just a young man I played a foolish game,
Told myself that something lost could never be regained,
Burned my bridges, smoked some hearts,
    quickly quit the chase,
Figured life wasn't worth the hurt
'cause she gone some other place.

Someone gave me whiskey and my head began to spin,
And something else they gave me got my thoughts to swim.
I tried to find her tracks one dawn by
    now there was no trace.
Even I can read the signs,
She gone some other place.

Life's a game of risk and I believe in fate and chance;
Every strange coincidence may lead to new romance.
Whatever it is you want, my friend, don't let it go to waste.
Rest assured you can beat the curse
When she's gone some other place.

Gray Sky Day

*It's a gray sky day
As we wait for rain,
Coffee's on the table,
It's a gray sky day.*

*The weatherman was wrong,
The cloud did not move on,
But I am not about to
Complain to you in song.*

*It's a gray sky day
As we wait for rain,
Coffee's on the table,
It's a gray sky day.*

*The children are upset.
What if their plans get wet?
Who are you to tell them
They have no need to fret?*

*And yesterday was dry
"Like tomorrow," you just sigh.
Oh, isn't it indeed a world
That makes you wonder why.*

*It's a gray sky day
As we wait for rain,
Coffee's on the table,
It's a gray sky day.*

Never Too Far

It's a town of minstrels and misery,
A place I swore I'd someday leave
Where the cat's got the dog up a tree
In good, ol' Westerly.

The railroad tracks still get used,
Corruption stains the daily news;
It's a town of chowder, beer and blues,
Old bounced checks and I.O.U.'s

Wherever it is I now roam
I'm never too far from home.

I can see her in my rearview mirror,
Summer nights when the coast was clear,
Before I washed away my tears,
And even now she is near.

Then those fools tore her down,
Pulled a rose from the ground;
Me, I couldn't stick around
But guess what I have found.

Wherever it is I now roam
I'm never too far from home.

So how come I'm back here again
Where I know every creak and bend,
Where lives begin to someday end
Forever rememberin'?

*When I feel that northeast wind
I know where I got started in,
Know where I'm goin' is where I been,
And I'll be back again.*

*Wherever it is I now roam
I'm never too far from home.*

Playing out at open mike nights in south Florida bars and clam shacks introduced me to the circus of wanna-be musicians all eager to be heard and appreciated. I met big egos and sincere beginners, hackers and hucksters, Deadheads and drunkards. One guy named Gino had a few good originals. One was called the "Dish Dog Blues." Then there was this Irish fellow Sean who was a beautiful guitar player with a huge folder of his own stuff.

My friend Paul Hitchon was the one who encouraged me to play my songs at these locales. Paul had lived a rather nomadic life and apparently found it difficult to keep in check his lust for life and women. He was a former wrestler and classically trained pianist who'd dedicated a good part of his life following the Grateful Dead. Somewhere along the line he'd picked up a guitar, and we seemed to click as a pair much in the same way I had with John and Joel. Paul's only problem was his unpredictable concentration on a performance, and I didn't help matters by often getting so nervous I forgot my own words. Of course there were some nights that made it all worthwhile, and then there were others I'd just as soon forget.

"It's the end of the world as we know it and I feel fine."
—R.E.M.

In my twenties I was as interested in writing protest songs as I was in trying to avoid the pitfalls of love. I wrote and still write mostly about both politics and love, but in my twenties I was much more specific. Later I learned how universal common experience is, but at the time I didn't know and honed in on whatever I was reacting to. "Runaway"'s three verses were mini-versions of stories about runaways in a local newspaper. "Tuesday Unemployment Line Rag" came directly from experience (in fact, the first half was written as I stood in line and Willie Nelson sang "You Were Always on My Mind" in the background) just as "Red Sox Fan" was a response to the '86 tragedy. These lyrics were immediate commentary.

Later lyrics seemed to evolve long after the fact. Lines and thoughts come from a deep well that I occasionally find the time and strength to tap. "Dirty Truth" was a reaction, but when I wrote it in early '91 I knew it was a culmination of several years in which I read scandal upon scandal in the papers and noticed I was drawn to such trash even though it repulsed me. "Caesar and Me" was written in haste after Joel had rattled my armor, but the chorus hummed itself to me the year before in San Rafael. "Montana Tom" came in two evenings, but I'd thought about him and a modern-day outlaw ballad ever since I met him in the winter of '87.

I've written dozens of songs about my wife. Some weren't meant for anybody but her to hear. A few of the others ("I Came For You", "Holy Love" and "Better Way to Be") appear in this collection, but sometimes what you write is only meant for yourself or one other person.

In the spring of '90 I started playing my songs in restaurants and liquor establishments. I played in a chapel, at a few parties, plenty of living rooms and, of course, a lot of garages. People always seemed to latch on to either story songs like "Mr. Meger's Store" or the "Red Sox" song, but my friends and musicians agreed "Cooper's Farewell" was the delivered goods. Personally there were some nights when I hated each and every song, then other nights when I was eager to just keep singing 'till the roosters crowed or the cops came or Neil Young phoned to ask us if anybody was being strangled . . .

Dirty Truth

Every day you wake up it's like another crash,
Somebody got caught it's a front page splash.
They treat you like royalty as they dig through your trash,
A little human decency is it too much to ask?

You can bitch and moan, cry it's unfair,
You can pay no attention, pretend it's not there,
Make like you're one of those people too cool to care,
You rubbernecking hypocrite, I saw you stare.

You may be Queen Rosie or Oldmaid Ruth,
I know you want to know about the dirty truth.

The media people, they've got a lot of gall,
Think they got the right to tell you it all,
Making something big out of something so small,
They'll raise you up just to watch you fall.

They say it's what you want, say it's what you need,
Helps take your mind off your own misery,
It's freedom of the press, freedom of speech,
Freedom to take away your privacy.

We've got our sources, we've got the proof,
Don't you want to know about the dirty truth?

Revelations shock as they titillate your brain,
Judgments are cast as fingers point blame.
It's all about cash, that's the name of the game,
When people smell money they have no shame.

There's a saying about a needle and a camel's eye,
An' the truly righteous people have nothin' to hide;
Seems nowadays even saints have a little sinner inside,
So who's your confidant, in whom do you confide?

They say one man's ceiling is another man's roof,
But how do you keep clean knowing the dirty truth?

Caesar and Me

What do you know? All I know is
I got hurt again,
Just when I thought I couldn't get caught,
I was in control and then

Funny how life seems to be like a spiral,
And it's always the same,
One day you think you got it all figured out,
But it don't really change.

And your dreams of skin are hung out to dry,
Don't you ever wish you didn't have to try
Don't you ever wish you didn't have to try

Where are you now? Oh, I don't know,
Where have you been?
Oh, I been around, even got out of town,
I got a taste for the wind.

Funny how you can't run away from yourself,
And there's really no place left to hide,
You're just going to have to face up to what it is
You got buried inside.

And your dreams of skin are hung out to dry,
Don't you ever wish you didn't have to try
Don't you ever wish you didn't have to try

What do you know? Hey, you think you got a hold
On how I really feel?
Think you know the road, the weight of my load,
How to spin my wheel?

Call it as you see it, dream and believe it,
You can paint your own world.
We made a little noise, we had some fun, boys,
So it went unheard.

And your dreams of skin are hung out to dry,
Don't you ever wish you didn't have to try
Don't you ever wish you didn't have to try

God Bless Us Now

The war machine has a fresh coat of green.
It's lookin' lean and clean like Bruce Springsteen.
Yeah, the pride is back, have yourself a Big Mac,
The train's on the track, ah yakkety yak.

Our boys are comin' home for every soldier that's unknown,
We're goin' to give them the greatest
    party man has ever thrown.

Our soldiers were brave as they awaited the day
The bombs we made would turn cities to graves,
So even if the news got you all confused,
One thing's for sure our boys didn't lose.

Our boys are comin' home for every soldier that's unknown,
We're goin' to give them the greatest
    party man has ever thrown.

So it's okay again to be an American.
If you've got an oil field we'll be your friend.
Get on the party line you deserve to feel fine,
Forget about the homeless 'till Christmas time.

Hail to the troops, man, you better salute,
Buy yourself some new Norman Schwarzkopf boots.
Wave your flags, don't let your bellies sag,
Put that ghost of Vietnam in a body bag.

Our boys are comin' home for every soldier that's unknown,
We're goin' to give them the greatest
    party man has ever thrown.

Nowadays

Everybody wants a piece of me
And everybody's so hard to please
Everybody prides themselves on praise
I doubt you could be humble
Nowadays

Possum played one too many cars
It's a game of inches stretched to yards
Call him road pizza, laugh at the waste
I don't understand
Nowadays

Sister don't know what she cannot feel
She been scratched enough to wear stainless steel
Too many people got their eyebrows raised
And still they're blind to what is
Nowadays

Nowadays
People can't smell
Nowadays
People can't taste
Nowadays
People can't tell
Even when
They're face to face

I used to believe in the wonder of skin
Now I can't get out of what I got myself in
I'm stuck in the mud to quote a phrase
And what will be already was
Nowadays

Everybody wants to give you advice
Everybody's got relief for a price
Seems you've got to follow a weird kind of maze
If you want to be a part of
Nowadays

Possum played one too many cars
It's a game of inches stretched to yards
Call him road pizza, laugh at the waste
I don't understand
Nowadays

Ballad of Montana Tom

Met a man named Montana Tom,
Who rolled into town before rollin' on,
Said he lived on the Indian land
Out there in Montana, man.
That's where he built himself a house
And that's where he met his wife,
The two of them blissful beatnik kids
About to start a new life.

Well they got into an argument,
And she went to town alone.
Tom was waiting to apologize,
But she wasn't comin' home.
It was snowing outside as she was driving
Nearly blind as the guy who was drunk;
Some people cannot win for losing,
And some people die too young.

Garbage on the reservation
While America dreams of Elvis Presley,
What's happened to your sensitivity, man?

Tom he headed for the borderline,
Kept headin' south escapeville time,
Went lookin' for Montezuma's tomb,
Walked upon the Aztec ruins,
Drank tequila and met a girl
Who was native to a natural world.
She was naked and free to touch
But not enough 'cause he still hurt too much.

So Tom he got back on the road,
loaded up with native clothes,

*enough to pay for the rent he hoped,
So he'd bum some meals and peddle some dope.
Wrote a road journal like Kerouac,
Psycho prose version of "Blood on the Tracks."
He still couldn't shake the hurt from his mind,
And he was lost across the borderline.*

*Garbage on the reservation
While America dreams of Elvis Presley,
What's happened to your sensitivity, man?*

*Tom ended up down at the beach
With his Guatemalan clothes and greeny weed.
He was trying to make a little money
Doin' his best to live off bummin'.
He played his soul on mandolin,
Told stories that stretched beneath your skin,
Then he went back to the Indian land
With whatever he had in his empty van.*

*My brother went out to visit him,
Said he lived high among drunk Indians.
Paranoia was thick in the air.
There was dirt in his beard, his eyes elsewhere.
Gypsy Teresa saw him in Frisco,
And he acted like she was someone he didn't know.
Maybe his eyes had just seen too much,
Or maybe his memory don't remember enough.
Sounds like he still goes from coast to coast,
Then back to Montana to walk the ghost,
Mandolin player Montana Tom
Who rolled into town before rollin' on.*

*Garbage on the reservation
While America dreams of Elvis Presley,
What's happened to your sensitivity, man?*

Full Circle

There's a road ahead full of valley dust and a pirate's song
And a thousand tales of sailors who one day just up and gone

And her twisted hope that romance could ever soothe his soul
As he breathes the wind and dances off the dirty, rotten cold

North by northeast south by west
Goin' full circle from now until the next
Call these rollin' hills of water my home
Salt for my wounds

There's a dark-eyed sky and maybe
    another shipwreck up ahead
A freight boat loaded up down at the
    docks, a sailor in her bed

She'd be a fool to believe in what he mumbled to her tonight
As he talked about the hardships there'd
    be come morning light

North by northeast south by west
Goin' full circle from now until the next
Call these rollin' hills of water my home
Salt for my wounds

They pulled into Portugal just around high tide
He met a dancing girl who invited him inside

She was in the desert where no sailor marks a tomb
He was in some diesel dump with a girl who owned a room

The wind was full of kerosene and the moon was on its way
As the old sea captain drank his due
    and talked about the grave

She moved on from town to town 'till she found the coast
Where she met a quiet man who did not believe in ghosts

Now he has to shake off the sweats as he gets up slow
He coughs out his own exhaust with one place left to go

She used to feel his tattoo as if a part of him
And with his back to her she'd dream of where he'd been

North by northeast south by west
Goin' full circle from now until the next
Call these rollin' hills of water my home
Salt for my wounds

Splitting Time: 1993-2000

Upon completing my first version of Scratchings, *I embarked on a decade-long journey of lyric writing and music making in two separate but equally important collaborations. The first involved my continuing work with Joel during the summer. For several more years, Vick and I returned to the converted garage on what was once my grandparents' property at Mastuxet Cove in Westerly. Vick painted water colors while I wrote; it was a beautiful bit of time. Joel would come by to try out my latest batch of songs, croquet games and barbeque parties grew into epic affairs, John Laprey and his wife Kari visited from Maine. My brother occasionally brought fresh fish, while my sister introduced her catch, the love of her life and eventual husband, Rand Richards Cooper, a novelist and vicious croquet player. We contributed our own terror to the mix, a wild young corgi we named MoJo, who treated us like cows or chow depending on what we were holding and how low we held it.*

By this time Joel had moved out of Crescent Street. His roomie Spencer one day announced, "My fifteen year summer vacation is over," and headed home to Tennessee. Joel found a new place not far from Misquamicut Beach, where he reassembled his home studio and recruited a band of players he dubbed Gravy Boat which included his brother Chip, Chris Chapman on drums, the ever steady and reliable Chris Rose on guitar, George Markham on bass, and eventually Tobe Kniffin, who would one day bring Joel on board as his band Green Tea's bass player.

By 1998 the Cove Years were behind us, but not before Joel and his crew helped me record Don't Give Me The Look. *From these sessions the Bob Marley tribute "Time to Live" would one day make it onto Green Tea's second CD* Steep. *"Sometimes It Takes All Night" came pouring out of me one night in the fever of a panic attack. It was a few years before death began to stalk my family, but I had this moment of dread one night while Vick was away visiting her dad. At this time Joel and I also co-wrote a song called "Gold Dust" which seemed to sum up more than just that end of summer feeling. Sometimes I feel as if I let him down not promoting that CD enough. I never committed fully to peddling my songs to publishers and other musicians. But no regrets now. You learn as you go. There was always my regular job as a teacher and another character down south who was tempting me to go in a stranger direction. So I split time and started writing a different kind of song.*

Last Sunday

Thought I saw you, yeah just for a second I
    thought I caught a glimpse of you
But the sun was out and it was a crowd of people
    last Sunday strolling on the avenue
There was the popcorn man and the carousel,
    young girls reveling in their wearwithall
And if only for an instant I thought I could envision it
Last Sunday I thought I saw you

Thought I knew you well enough so that even if
    I had to guess I could expect to be right
But it's always a mystery even as the experience
    teaches us about the distance out there tonight
There's a young girl in the tea room reminds me
    of a time to come long gone too soon
And if only for an instant just to have
    myself another glimpse of it
Last Sunday I thought I saw you

Thought I heard your voice one night but when
    I looked outside nobody was there
I've travelled a long way now not to think hey
    I might not have gotten anywhere
We've all got our shadows of doubt and this
    I know a thing or two about
And if only for an instant if I could just
    have back a glimpse of it
Last Sunday I thought I saw you

Holy Love

When I first met you you seemed so
    calm and full of quiet bliss
It never would have dawned on me that something was amiss
Your almond eyes were watching me I
    could feel them all the time
You spoke to me of your dreams as you slipped inside of mine
Then you took me home and I didn't leave 'till dawn
Haunted by old love affairs with a new one comin' on

Something in me tugged and pulled and tied me up in knots
I hit the road, went back home, found out I was lost
You were there beside me when I was alone inside my dream
And before I tried to explain myself you
    knew just what it'd mean
You even told me to go suffer if it'd help me write a song
You can't depend on something so old it
    can't see a new one comin' on

We drifted apart like people do then
    we got back together again
Took a good look at our situation, those
    driftin' days were now to end
You had this look in your eyes that said this is meant to be
And after looking around myself it finally dawned on me
Now you look out the window at the sun upon the lawn
The old days are over we've got new ones comin' on

There's a power of loneliness
There's a power of holy love
There's a power of loneliness
There's a power of holy love

Rome, Italy

John Keats died while still in love
Even as he lay there coughing up blood
He loved and tended to his sickly mother
He also cared for his dying brother
Then he died down in Rome, Italy

John Keats was supposed to be a doctor
But he could not bear becoming an imposter
He decided to make writing his life
Despite the hardship and financial strife
He thought it noble to become a poet
Just like all those guys down in Rome, Italy

And as he lay dying in bed
His friend drew a picture of him
He thought his name was written in water
But his words still blow in the wind

He wrote a poem about a nightingale
How beauty is truth as he got sick and pale
He poured his soul into all that he wrote
And dedicated his life to being a poet
Before he died down there in Rome, Italy
Before he died down there in Rome, Italy

John Keats loved a girl named Fanny Brawne
And his love for her was like the light of dawn
But he also loved and cared for his mother
And he stayed by the side of his dying brother
And then he died down there in Rome, Italy
That's where he's buried now in Rome, Italy

And as he lay dying in bed
His friend drew a picture of him
He thought his name was written in the water
But his words still blow in the wind

Sometimes It Takes All Night

Couple of friends of mine
Said they were gonna stop on by
When I see it I'll have my proof
Yeah sometimes these things take awhile
You gotta let the distance gather some miles
Old friends never take long to renew

But then you spin in the dusty wind
And turn to see your shadow again
Fadin' into the glimmering light,
You know you've got to carry yourself
Beyond where it is you used to dwell
Sometimes it takes all night

Well it's rags to riches back to rags again
The road rolls on until you get to the end
Sometimes you've got to stop to take a break,
But other times there's no getting off
You've got to find your own bridge to cross
And gather up what you've got left to lose or make

But out there in the howling rain
An old ghost rattles and pulls your chain
You wish the lightning would surely come to strike,
And damned if you know who's to tell
What it is that makes you well
Sometimes it takes all night

There's a fire down by the cove
A heap of ashes in the woodstove
A letter to you I wrote and burned
About a kid who got pumped up
And then of course he got dumped
Everybody's equal when it comes their turn

But now inside the dry dead heat
I sweat the old hurt out of me
And your wet eyes say it's all right
And c'est la vie if all's not well
I know you'll save me from myself
Even if it takes all night
Sometimes it takes all night

How do I put this delicately? My other musical project of the '90's involved pairing up with another reclusive musician do-it-yourselfer who conspired to build the ultimate home studio and mischievously dubbed us the....well, suffice it to say he was a master of sexual innuendo and he often referred to me as a "bonehead" when it came to understanding the intricacies of the studio set up. So you, good reader, can figure it out from there. I'll admit our moniker was very punk and a perfect extension of what rock 'n roll and the early rhythm and blues implied to curious youth and mortified adults alike. It led Rob to conjur up a million different CD titles. He joked that our Johnny Cash prison album would be Doing Hard Time, *while our concert set would be called* Live from Morey's Lounge, *referring to a notoriously low end gentleman's establishment. Meanwhile, Rob began collecting old analog equipment, including an eight track one inch reel to reel Atari that supposedly once belonged to the Bee Gees. He had this old Leslie cabinet speaker, a Mackie mixer, and more and more processors and drum machines as we went along. We often composed songs on the spot, or Rob would build tracks while staying up all night and later I would add vocals. The nine year project was experimental by nature; fueled on various English ales, we composed songs about the OJ trial,* The X-Files, *pin-up girls, presidential pizza parties. At one point Rob was renting a house and brought over a drummer and bass player who he conveniently placed along with me and our expensive Audio-Technica microphone in a room separated from him and the recording equipment. We proceeded to make some wild Stooges-style noise that destroyed the mic but was cathartic on some level for me. At that session I was making up lyrics on the spot, and in the middle of a song called "Owed," I apparently vented about my job:*

"You see there's circles and squares, they just turn you into little things, and they put you in your place, they put you in your place, they make you sit down and look at them with a straight face, that's what they do, they do that to you, they do that to you. I don't think it's fair, I don't think it's right, I don't think it's right, I don't think it's right so

I cruise along the avenue, I cruise with myself, I cruise with myself, I listen to Patti Smith and I cruise with myself, I listen to Patti Smith and I cruise with myself, I listen to Patti Smith and I cruise with myself."

Later in the song I find myself confessing what the experience of music making means to me:

"This is where we go when we have to get small
and we get back our senses. You know, the child in us all,
we get ourselves down in this primordial ooze, this is where
we get it, this is where we get the pre-generation blues,
you know the music, you know the music,
   you know the music, we know it

After hours is always open, after hours is always open
The universe is expanding and our home is broken
but we can reach out, we can find it, we can get in that space,
you find that place, you find that place."

I certainly found it with Rob. Six months later he was looking after his mom at her apartment in Lake Worth. He moved in with his studio and was able to continue quietly recording wild, raucous music under headphones. His childhood friend Mike Sullivan occasionally visited from Maryland. A beautiful soul and mean guitar player, Mike encouraged Rob to bring the project to fruition. Songs such as "Alien Soul" might have been larks, but "Lighthouse","Watching the Waves" and "Iron Love" hinted at Rob's brilliance. Despite his perfectionist ways, even he sensed that we were close to putting something truly magical together.

And then life caught up to us. Rob's mom got very ill, and he shut the studio down to dutifully and lovingly tend to her. I, meanwhile, battled tinnitus for the next few years and a bout of Epstein-Barr, both of which helped me develop a healthier lifestyle with its own benefits. After going our separate ways for awhile, Rob and I found our way back to playing some guitar together, and I hope someday he dusts off those old reel to reel tapes and lights up that Atari again.

Watching the Waves

I watch myself disappear everyday now
I become a little more invisible
I check myself out in the mirror
I smile all the while I am miserable

Watching the waves
I wish I could be out there today
Watching the waves
Oh man, I wish I could be
Out there today

Light shimmers on the water
The sky grows quiet now
There's no need for recognition
when nobody else is around

Watching the waves
Watching the waves

I got an ego the size of Picasso
I believe in those who dream
about the impossible
Yeah, right now I've got blue glass
and skies of rose

Watching the waves, man the time flows

Alien Soul

I've been buttressed by your alien soul
I know there's a God in that big black hole
I know there's beauty in the darkest picture
I know there's something better than the latest mixture

What do you think they're putting in the water?
What do you think's making you not want to bother?
Is the color that good on your television set
Makes you not even want to think about
    what you'd just as soon
forget?
I've been told that the universe expanded
At exactly the hour God commanded;
You are free to believe but never not to abandon
The truth is out there but do you dare try
    to find out where it landed?

Spooky Fox Mulder says he wants to believe
But the only one he trusts is agent Dana Scully
He wants to find his sister in the light beyond the darkness
Meanwhile trying to solve all sorts of unexplained phenomena
Parasites from outer space and devil disciples
Government conspiracies and inexplicable mysteries
All forms of paranormal activity
Disfigured products of the X-Ray Generation
In a world where everybody is under investigation
And shadows tell secrets and give you a piece of the truth
And you know how the evidence can be so hard to prove

I'm pulling for you Mulder to find your sister
Or at least I hope they let you go and visit her;
They must think us sadly funny and oddly strange
And marvel at how we never seem to change
Pity this poor child monster mankind
Who seeks in himself what he cannot help but find
I still believe we are here because He planned it
The truth is out there I hope to understand it
Yeah, the truth is out there, let's go find out where it landed

Lighthouse

I wake up every morning with sweat in my eyes
I tell you it's time I've got to realize
I aint getting any younger
If you're into counting numbers
I've got to get with the program
Before I'm sold into not being who I am

I've been obstructed by the same old crowd
I've been abducted and disavowed
I aint getting any smarter
Though maybe I'm a little harder
Harder to follow
Harder to swallow
Don't choke on yourself

Everything is possible where I come from
You've just got to figure out a way to get it done
And dreams are like…good rain
The taste of freedom and love unchained
I'm with you no matter what they say
'cause you know the world's going to come around
And tell you to do things its way
There's not a lot of room for flexibility
People get lazy
Everybody has good intentions
But then they get carried away with their inventions
It always equals more or less
Progress

Break out while you can
Go with the flow, let the rhythm be your friend
I saw you dancing like everything's gonna be better
Than it's ever been
Don't let those shadows get under your skin
Break out while you can

Nobody Else

I wake up in the blank grey
Of one more industrial day
My girlfriend's mood could go either way
I really don't feel like I have that much to say
So I walk down Crescent Street
With easy walker shoes on my feet
And the same pants you patched up for me
So only you knew about my knobby knees

If only you knew how I felt
Or never would about nobody else

Then I discovered Jonathan
In the cut out record bins
And Little Jerry who took me in
She said, "It's who you are
not who you been."
So I raise my flag of skull and bones
I'm not afraid to be alone
I'm comin' back to where I once was goin'
I used to rock but now I just roll

If only you knew how I felt
Or never would about nobody else

Before I put on the miles
To get to my tropic isle
I clothed myself in your hand me down smile
I almost felt safe for just a little while
I'm still looking for something to spin
All my salvation used to be the record bins
When I was outside looking in
'cause who I am is who I been

If only you knew how I felt
Or never would about nobody else

Hey To Your Sister

It gets hard, love, bridging the distance
Connecting the lines we crossed
Picking up the pieces
Reconciling the loss

It takes a sturdy constitution
A little hair of the dog
A touch of rebel rousing music
A healthy respect for the law

Say hey to your sister and old Mr. Larry
I'm feelin okay now if anybody queries
I've ripped myself up before
But you've always repaired me

I understand why nobody listens
The air's too full of sound
It's a sad day, a sad situation
When you teach yourself to put yourself down

It's a hard time to seek forgiveness
Especially when they think that you're wrong
They're gonna drive you into indifference
And stake a knife into your song

Say hey to your sister and old Mr. Larry
I'm feeling okay now if anybody queries
I've ripped myself up something good
But you've always repaired me

It gets hard, love, bridging the distance
Connecting the lines we crossed
Picking up the pieces
Reconciling the loss

I understand why nobody listens
The air's too full of sound

*"One good thing about music
when it hits you feel no pain"*
—*Bob Marley*

Fiddle Me A River: 2001-2009

In the spring of 1999 Vick, MoJo and I moved to Lake Worth. We bought a 50's era concrete block house and busied ourselves making a home. Lake Worth turned out to be a quirky town quickly becoming populated by Mayan families and young gay couples. Its history was rich and dark, a one time settlement homesteaded by ex-slaves Samual and Fanny James. Fanny was reportedly a part Seminole black woman who named the area Jewel and, after losing her husband, sold the property to some outside developers. After her mysterious death as supposedly one of south Florida's first automobile fatalities, the area was divided into little plots and advertised as a "whites friendly" town named after Seminole-disposer General William J. Worth. It would later become home to a Grand Wizard of the Ku Klux Klan. Bad juju all around.

Some of life's harsher realities started paying regular visits. Vick's business was practically stolen from her and left her uprooted; my beloved grandmother passed away soon followed by news of my brother's cancer. After a brave two year battle, he succumbed, and not so long after Vick's dad started failing. But you can always find balance, and there were moments of pure redemptive light: my sister marrying Rand and later giving birth, the Red Sox finally winning a World Series, friends such as Fred Buffum and John Laprey staying married and raising families. As much as we share what is lost, we also find solace in the gentler moments. I choose to believe it all equals out.

As always I kept on writing lyrics, sometimes fashioning them into songs. By this point they were mostly autobiographical, my documentation of a people, time and place and how I felt about them. Brother's illness, grandmother's spirit, my ever growing appreciation of my wife's patience and persistence, the miraculous distraction of the 2004 baseball season. There was even a magical two day recording session with Joel and Chappy one December when I was up in Rhode Island visiting family. As Marley sang, "We can carry on."

Seabird

She head for the hills and didn't come back
Now I miss what I didn't know I had
Maybe we'll meet up ahead
And dance a jig in dawn's sweet breath

I believe in the grace of God
I believe in no man's law
I believe in wind and rain
And all that was shall be again

Five loaves of bread and two good fish
Ocean road and salty mist
Dreams and memory all in one
What is gone is yet to come

Now Grandma lies alone in bed
Most days that's as far as she gets
She wants me to bring her books on ghosts
She wants to see one before she goes

Watch the seabird as she flies
Into the greywhite hazy skies
Maybe we'll meet up ahead
And dance a jig in dawn's sweet breath

Mastuxet Cove

When I was a little kid I found an arrowhead
Lying beneath some maple leaves on my granddad's property
Must have been from long ago in the days before the roads
When the seasons came on slow down along Mastuxet Cove
Every fall we'd build a fort and have a
    horse chestnut and apple war
No one ever got that hurt and there's
    nothing wrong with a little dirt

Then the years came along and took
    me down this road I'm on
For awhile I got off track, closed my eyes and turned my back
But I kept in touch with my old friends and
    eventually I would visit them
Every chance I would return to rekindle
    flames already burned
'cause any spark that might ignite might
    produce a piece of light
Of the fires burned long ago down along Mastuxet Cove

In summers kids from Connecticut drive
    down to Misquamicut
Where the clam shacks open up again
    and the girls get on their
coconut skin
Knowing full well in a couple months all
    the shops will be boarded up
And the wind will come in cold and
    raw blow sand across empty
parking lots
'cause seasons come and seasons go say
    so long to the summer folk
Once again time gets slow like it used to be on Mastuxet Cove

My memories get entwined with what
　　I seek to eventually find
Pride and vanity, fish and beer, the fog
　　rolls in eyes can only hear
I try to write it down in song, half the
　　time it comes out wrong
I know there's many rules of thumb and the good Lord's work
Is never done
And the poet's path is the open road but
　　nothin's deep as being home
Where water drifts and sun sets low like
　　a quiet fire on Mastuxet Cove

Nostalgia is a yellow mood and mine is more a grayish blue
The boathouse smell of salt and mold,
　　August nights of almost cold
"Remember children throughout your lives
　　there's nothing better than
A good surprise."
Dog days, old brown eyes, "It's alright, Ma…
　　don't think twice."
Sister, brother, father, mother, never again to be lovers
Grandma searching for a ghost home is where the river flows

All I Know

So many things can happen at once
All I know's the need for love
Don't ever go away
And the sun shines down on the lonely and brave
The flash of neon and the sky of smoke
And all the words that man ever wrote
So many things can happen at once
All I know's the need for love

I watch the moonlight slip away
In that time between night and day
Your love has always been
Some place I know I can get to again

Not much left of the good old days
But tomorrow's got its own tale to chase
All the numbers only equal so much
All I know's the need for love

All the sadness you ever fought
That lifelong lesson about Murphy's Law
They say faith can heal a man
But first you've got to give a damn
Every rose blooms and fades
And no good story ever goes to waste
So many things can happen at once
All I know's the need for love

I watch the moonlight slip away
In that time between night and day
Your love has always been
Some place I know I can get to again

Late August

I've seen you walking out in the cold
Watching the birds fly off in a sky of burnt gold
I can handle the weather when the seasons change
But I don't know if I can face the darkness again

You can see a whole lot the more that you look
And life will teach you as much as you
    might get out of some book
But it sure helps to know what others have had to say
And I'd only be half of who I am without
    the people I met along the way

And I couldn't even imagine ever
    passing through without you

Once I was dropped off on the side of the road
In the middle of nowhere with miles and miles to go
I could have waited for some ride that might never come
But instead I decided to walk in your direction

And I didn't know for sure if you'd be there
So I told myself it was pointless to even care
But sometimes you find the light out of the blue
And I aint going anywhere now without you

And I couldn't even imagine ever
    passing through without you

There's all sorts of propositions and choices to make
And you're gonna find out if you can
    be good for goodness sake
Maybe you'll succeed more than you fail
Maybe you'll see the light at the end of the trail

Maybe you'll find yourself back out on the road
Singing your own version of the oldest story ever told
There's so many lies, a few simple truths
No man is worthless but I'm nothing without you

Yeah, I couldn't even imagine ever
  getting through without you

Dog Beach

Every morning I hum my devotion
As I watch the sun rise out of the ocean
I think of ol' Pete the pirate
How he used to surf off Dog Beach in the twilight

So I go back and turn around
Hit the highway headin' south
Gunnin' it to the land of palm fronds
Boats full of whiskey and bon vie bon
Shady tree boys and barefoot girls
Dirty beach shack pretty white pearl
Bleached by the sun and raised in the surf
She lives down at the last block at the end of the universe

Lots of gift shops where the Seminoles used to live
And runaway slaves escaped to and hid
Where famous folk would come down to fish
And watch the night sky for the light of rocket ships

I still think of my old friend John
How he used to watch the moon in the early hours of dawn
Then he'd catch the wind and go for a ride
There wasn't nothing Johnny wouldn't try

Now there's buildings taking up every inch of land
Buildings in the swamp, buildings right up to the sand
Living behind gates feeling secure and safe
And that big blue sky is now a golden brown haze

There's not much left of how it once was
'cept I heard Chief Billy's back to building chikki huts
Even if every silver lining's got a touch of grey
That old river's gonna find its own way

Every morning I hum my devotion
Quiet time before the daily commotion
You can still see ol' Pete surfing off Dog Beach
And once in a while you can catch a whiff of the old days
in the breeze

Better Way to Be

Got to admit I'm shaky, the world can spin so fast
Every moment's precious but nothing is meant to last
I hold on to you each night as I drift off to sleep
For all the bad I might have done you found the good in me
Life aint always pleasant it's toil sometimes for naught
There aint no rhyme nor reason nor equality of law
But you smiled out to me
And taught me a better way to be

Cut me slack you give me rope enough to hang myself
And when I looked down I saw the sky
   at the bottom of the well
Irish poets in the moonlight and rain-soaked Rasta girls
It's a big old universe for such a small world
Devil's in the details but God's got a touch of soul
Greatest preacher I ever heard used to
   play a mean rock 'n roll
And you smiled out to me
And taught me a better way to be

Remember that trip down the mountain
   how you just about collapsed
And when you got back home you realized
   your future wasn't a thing of the past
There was a rainbow in your backyard
   and a dog who taught you love
You've got to hold onto your grace despite all that other stuff
Kid asked me if I was chillin' like Bob
   Dylan I had to laugh to myself
When you look down can you see the
   sky at the bottom of the well
Yeah, you smiled out to me
And taught me a better way to be

Ballad of the Boston Red Sox Fan (Part Two)

Man, it's been many a year since I wrote this song,
Many a World Series have come and gone.
Now we're in a whole new era
With Pedro and Manny and Garciaperra
Still tryin' to beat the Curse
And catch the Yankees who are always in first.

Hope springs eternal every March
And life goes on despite broken hearts.
The Red Sox have taught me about dealing with grief
And how faith can run into disbelief.
You can't give up no matter what;
There aint no shaking a kid's first love.

So there we were in 2004
Once again knocking on the door.
The Yankees beat us in games one, two, three
Then along came David Ortiz
Who helped us win games four and five
And what do you know we were still alive.
Then Schilling came on stitched and soar
And showed us what we paid him all that money for,
And despite a season of slump and strife
Derek Lowe pitched the game of his life,
And Johnny Damon found his stroke,
And as God is my witness it was the Yankees who choked,
I'm a Red Sox fan.

So what can I say maybe it was in the stars.
We didn't fold against the mighty Cards.
These idiots got it right
And played the game with a kid's delight.
Ah, to live long enough to live a lifelong dream,
To raise my glass to a championship team,
To dance with my cap in hand
And smile all winter as a Red Sox fan.

Deeper Shade of Grey

I saw an owl in the morning light;
The thought alone filled me with delight.
Could be Wes just checking in.
I had to laugh
There goes ol' Grandma again.
Later that day I learned I might lose my room;
That's okay I'll just have to move.
Little black cat crossed my path.
Before disappearing she slowly looked back.
Made me think of Satchel Paige
Pitching in the twilight of his career
At the dawn of a new age
When the starlight still lit the way
And everything was a deeper shade of grey.

The storms of life are cruel and blind.
You never know what you may happen to find.
You can look at yourself as hard as you can,
And you still may not know enough to understand.
The only thing I wish I'd said
Is something I didn't quite get to instead.
Don't look back it'll only bring you down
Or spring you loose from where you thought you were bound.
Just where that is I'm not sure anyways.
I'm a bit unnerved, rattled and frayed.
Perhaps that's the price of a deeper shade of grey.

The days get mixed up in memory and dream.
A couple of times we wiped the slate clean
Like that time we drove all night to catch the Dead.
I can still see those hills in the morning light ahead.
As the leaves would fall you'd breathe the air and grin
And cast out your line for some refuge in the wind.
Souls don't die they shine on within.
That's what I'm tryin' my best to believe in.
The channel bell clangs, rocks and sways.
Time's not lost it's just on its way
And I'm still here in this deeper shade of grey.

Back in the Ocean State

A big old storm came ashore in 1938
It took down houses left and right in one gigantic wave
I wasn't born yet hell my dad was just a babe
But the story's been handed down and
    it's still walking around today
One foot in the Ocean State

Used to ride these roads in old Mabe my Chevrolet
Right by the graveyard where the ghostboy used to play
The salt on my tongue and wind in my face
Takes me back to another time and place
Back in the Ocean State

Where my name was writ in water and shadows fill up space
Back in the Ocean State

I took the road less traveled so I could find my own way
And here I am thinking about that old storm from '38
People built their homes back up and somehow kept the faith
You give up what you got to and do whatever it takes
Takes me back to the Ocean State

Some folks made enough money to hang on to their estates
And some folks just aint making it no
    matter how much they scrimp
And scrape
Some folks dig their roots so deep they can't escape
Ah, but envy, don't give me your sour grapes
I'm washing my mouth out in the Ocean State

Yeah, a big old storm came to shore in 1938
It took down houses far and wide but
  somehow the fort remained
It's nothing but weeds out there and poison ivy nowadays
The cackle of seabirds and lapping of waves
On the shores of the Ocean State

Jamaican Nights

There's a quarter moon between the telephone wires
One night last June when your voice was on fire
It was rainy and cold, the guitars entwined
I was around old friends and everything was fine
'till the next day come and you know
    what the next day brings
You live long enough you'll know about
    that stuff that the bluesman
sings
Yeah, they tell me Rome was not built in a day
And I tell 'em right back some things never go away

and the stars in the sky are so clear up
    on high Jamaican nights
yeah the stars in the sky are so clear up
    on high Jamaican nights

I come to drink from where the water runs deep
And try to catch a bit of the wind that you used to breathe
The rooster knows it's mornin' my belly knows it too
Junior says the doctor breeze gonna meet the undertaker soon
I saw Georgie sittin' on the steps of the Hope Road house
And a bunch of Bob's children just hangin' out
There's garbage in the streets, kids playin' soccer in the yard
Even if the road's your home it's good
    to come home to where you
know who you are

and the stars in the sky are so clear up
    on high Jamaican nights
yeah the stars in the sky are so clear up
    on high Jamaican nights

We stopped in Woody's place to have us some cheer
Some smiles say hello, others say,"What are you doing here?"
It was a Thursday night there was no music going on
But even the quiet around here is its own kind of song
So I took time out from the rule of man
I held her soft skin in my hand
Thoughts came to me from a long ways away
Time will tell but will you hear what it has to say?

and the stars in the sky are so clear up
   on high Jamaican nights
yeah the stars in the sky are so clear up
   on high Jamaican nights

Our whole Jamaica experience has been like something out of a dream. My brother-in-law pulled a magazine assignment to research and write about the history of jerk seasoning, and so he and my sister, Vick and I tagging along, ventured to Boston Beach near Port Antonio, Jamaica late December of 2003. On the last day of our stay there, I dragged Vick to the Bob Marley Museum on Hope Road in Kingston. We met Georgie of "No Woman, No Cry" fame, and Vick flashed on the notion that Marley's music and message were kindred spirits to her own Montessori-based peace education efforts. Not long after returning from Jamaica, Vick received a call from Rita Marley's daughter Sharon who was on hiatus from the Melody Makers and running a day care center in Kingston. She inquired about Vick's Montessori training center in Miami, and thus began their partnership as peace education crusaders.

Vicki and I have been back a number of times since then. A few summers ago we left Treasure Beach two days before Hurricane Dean whalloped the area. Something keeps luring us back. The heat is different in Jamaica. There's the trade winds for one thing, the undertaker and doctor breeze. It's an island with a turbulent history and pockets of brutal poverty, yet it is also a land of profoundly natural beauty and independent-minded people. Up in the mountains and along the northeast coast you really can sense "a natural mystic blowing through the air." Marley tapped into it, and I've often experienced great imaginings while listening to his rhythmic songs.

A dozen years earlier I sat at my friend John Laprey's dining table on a sweltering hot July day in Cape Neddick, Maine and typed out the lyrics for "Time to Live." It was my tribute to Marley written after reading Timothy White's Catch A Fire. *I would go on to write songs paying my respects to a number of the people who inspired me to write and play music: Carl Sandburg, Maya Angelou, the street singer Ted Hawkins, my college mentor Hugh Ogden, John Hartford, and, most recently, the unsurpassable Odetta, though I'm having trouble editing that one. I never could finish a fitting tribute to Dylan either, maybe because you cannot force these pieces; they have to come of their own accord.*

Time to Live

*Bob Marley on Sunday sounds as good as he does on Friday
That's why I like that music wherever I happen to be
He had to root it out, pull on its
   sustenance, survive in Jamaica
How many of you will ride your lives as far as it will take ya?*

*Time's a trickster and tricks are for kids
It's kind of like your first goodnight kiss
Slap yourself, buddy, wake up kid
You've got nothin' but time to live*

*Rasta man with his good vibration, his
   sacred herb and his ring
of Solomon
Miami night in a concrete hospital, but
   "You cannot bury Jah, mon!"
Mr. Tough Gong play me a "Redemption
   Song" from your island house
to your shack in Trenchtown
Bob Marley on Sunday sounds as good as he does on Friday*

*Hello moonlight, sun on the horizon
The dead live on every morning we be risin'
Slap yourself, buddy, wake up kid
You've got nothin' but time to live*

*"After this I looked up and before my eyes was a door open up
to Heaven and a voice speaking to me
   like a trumpet, said, 'Come
here, I'll show you what must happen hereafter'."*

*Bob Marley on Sunday sounds as good as he does on Friday
Bob Marley on Sunday sounds as good as he does on Friday*

Into Hope (Maya Angelou)

I've heard you know why the caged bird sings,
The sounds of silence sorrow brings,
I heard you broke free upon angel wings
And soared inside of you.

Where do you put what your heart hates to know?
How do you take the pain and make it into hope?
Maya Angelou

Stripped away from your ma and your pa,
Sent down river to Arkansas
Where God couldn't save you from man's law
But that aint nothin' new.

Then it happened when you were eight.
He got your body but your soul escaped.
You could have grown up one more victim of hate,
But God's love stuck in you.

Where do you put what your heart hates to know?
How do you take the pain and make it into hope?
Maya Angelou

They say the phoenix rose from the ash,
The future is only as close as the past,
Forgiveness is the hardest thing to ask.
You've got a lot inside of you.

You didn't just stop, you decided to go
Follow the river wherever it'd flow,
Every baby born's got a right to grow,
There's just so much a body can do.

Where do you put what your heart hates to know?
How do you take the pain and make it into hope?
Maya Angelou

I've heard you know why the caged bird sings,
The sounds of silence sorrow brings,
I heard you broke free upon angel wings
And soared inside of you.

So Are You (Ballad to Carl Sandburg)

Sandburg was a socialist
And a friend to the underdog,
He knew the good of common folk
And both ends of the law.

He knew the rhythm of the road,
The rail and the wind,
He knew about how flowers grow
To die and grow again.

"My aim's to sing and blab and chortle,
And yodel too…
I am the people…"
So are you

Sandburg failed his grammar test,
He also failed at math,
So he got his education
Takin' a different path.

He travelled 'cross the country,
Even rode the rails,
He hobnobbed with the hobos,
Spent some time in jail.

"My aim's to sing and blab and chortle,
And yodel too…
I am the people…"
So are you

*Sandburg was a journalist
And a social democrat,
Robert Frost called him a fraud
'cause his verse would skit and skat.*

*He wrote about Abe Lincoln
And the power of the vote,
He inspired Bobby Dylan
And Marilyn Monroe.*

*Sandburg died in '67
When the country was a mess,
But in that time of crazy change
Some people were their best.*

*Sandburg spoke of wisdom
And the promise that he saw,
He knew the truth of beauty
And both ends of the law.*

*"My aim's to sing and blab and chortle,
And yodel too…
I am the people…"
So are you*

*He wrote about Chicago,
Autumn, dawn, and jazz,
He wrote about the virtue
Of an innocence that lasts.*

*Sandburg wrote of rhythm,
The road, rail and wind,
He knew about how flowers grow
To die and grow again.*

*"My aim's to sing and blab and chortle,
And yodel too…
I am the people…"
So are you.*

Hammer Man (To Hugh Ogden)

I can see you with a hammer in your hand
Walking across this proud old land.
The sky is grey and hard times are on their way,
But you've got that hammer in your hands.

Life don't always work out how you had it planned.
One moment you're blessed, the next you're damned.
You make out of it what you can.
I can see you with a hammer in your hand.

Shades of light cut deep lines,
Grief and joy are the ties that bind,
But it's the work itself that defines a man.
I can see you with a hammer in your hand.

Truth be told it's grim out there.
You can point your finger just about anywhere.
The news drones on, it's a deathly hum.
It makes you wonder where people are coming from.

Fear reaps what it sows in man.
Sometimes I feel too much to understand.
I saw you hurting from love like any man.
Then I saw you holding a hammer in your hand.

I can see you with a hammer in your hand
Walking across this fertile land.
The sky is grey and hard times are on their way,
But you've got that hammer in your hand.

Yeah, you've got that hammer in your hand.
Yeah, you've got that hammer in your hand.

*Shades of light cut deep lines,
You can create your own world and mark the time,
And build a road to the heart of man,
I can see you with a hammer in your hand.*

Woody Guthrie's Dog (To MoJo)

My dog doesn't understand private property
She just lets her nose show the way,
She sure don't act like the Queen's dog
Maybe she's got Indian DNA

My dog knows a bunch of words, she's
    partial to "dinnertime"
She's got the patience of a farmer's daughter
    and the eyebrows of old
Einstein,
And she's got a touch of Jack Nicholson
    when I ask her to come
But most of all she just likes to…bark and run

My dog will roll in stuff strong enough
    to make a grown man moan
She likes to chase motorcycles and curl up
    on the couch with her bone
Yeah, she's got a mind of her own for
    sure, she's a little rebel with
paws
Doesn't pay no mind to park ordinances
    or care much for man's leash
laws
I don't think she's too partisan, if you're liberal or neocon,
As long as you're feeding the needy and she's one of 'em
She don't care which side you're on

She's a good traveling companion, loyal as they come
But it's tough being a prisoner of the suburbs
Sometimes she's just got to bark and run

You know I wonder if I should take her to a farmer
Who's got a head of cattle to herd
She could boss around cows all day long
Be happy with a hard day's work

Yeah, we live in these little boxes with
*   our schedules and routines*
Hooked on fast food news and all the latest madmen schemes
But everyday when I get home my dog
*   licks my face and hands*
She wags what would be a tail and smiles to beat the band
I'm going to end this song on an old-fashioned positive note
'cause like Woody Guthrie once said,
*   "A song should give a man*
some hope."

Fascists and oilmen will come and go
People keep dreaming, dreams do grow
So strum your guitar, brother, sister, bang your drum
And don't forget to let your dog out to bark and run

Terror and Love

Isn't it amazing how you can get so far
From Parchman Farm to Pico Boulevard
From those dark nights inside four white walls
Amazing what you know when you've got nothing at all
Used to see you on the beach on your crate
Strumming 'till the strings on your
    guitar would almost break
Sand in your throat, holes in your shoes
You always found the soul inside the blues

Never brushed off your Delta dust
Deep in that voice there always was
Deep in that voice there was terror and love

The songs you sung you made your own
You sang of love like it was your home
The bitter fruit you find in life
The wrong turns you take trying to get it right
Used to see you out by Venice Beach
Singing as sweet and hard as you please
Sand in your throat, holes in your shoes
You always found the soul inside the blues

Never brushed off your wanderlust
Deep in that voice there always was
Deep in that voice there was terror and love

My daddy said accept a man for who he is
And then try to find the good in him
This I believe to be the truth
Most people are there to be kind to you
But people also got this need to eat
And it's dog eat dog that put the bark in me
So if you don't mind I will quench my thirst
And try as I might to write another verse

We all need something to trust
Deep in that voice there always was
Deep in that voice there was terror and love

Fiddle Me A River

John John the steamboat's gone but bless
    my soul the river rolls on
Around the creek up past the bend where
    everything old is new again
Slap that fiddle, play that lick, blow your
    horn when the fog gets thick
Remember how Huck helped his friend
    Jim; I'd like to think I would
have done like him.

There's a hard luck story everywhere you
    go and river towns full of
Do-si-do
And when the law's wrong it aint no sin to
    help a man find his family again.
John John the steamboat's gone but bless
    my soul the river rolls on

If the songs of God are writ in wood and wind
You know John's fiddlin' up in Heaven, my friend
Fiddlin' a tune to make you laugh
And help you catch up to the past

Every generation's got its Kings and
    Dukes, senseless crazy family
feuds,
Poets and singers who soothe the soul
    and warm you up when the
wind blows cold,
and kids who dream of river boats and don't mind puttin' on
hand-me-down clothes,
old men skipping in the morning dew kicking up dust as you
fiddle a tune

so who's that sittin' on the porch tonight
singin' high and lonesome in the blue moon light,
must be the ghost of old Huck Finn,
everything old is new again

John John the steamboat's gone but bless
    my soul the river rolls on
John John the steamboat's gone but bless
    my soul the river rolls on

The folk music I absorbed sitting on my daddy's knee still flows in me. The secret whisper of rock 'n' roll my best company. Reggae my spirit lifter. Some feelings you just can't fit into words. I find it hard explaining what's already been written anyway.

Songs get tossed around a lot. I've depended on the durable flexibility of many an old tune twisted around by my own awkward phrasing. I was either ridiculously cursed or awfully fortunate to be around when Dylan, Van, Creedence, the Stones, Arlo and countless others strung their words and melodies together. It got me to thinking in weird rhythmic patterns.

Maybe that snowy evening in the dead of some otherwise forgotten winter when I watched for the only time Odetta in flowing dress and big guitar sing unrecognizable words in a voice that told me more than I could ever know. . . maybe that was when I really gave up writing poetry for a life of lyrics. Went back and wrote "Runaway" shortly after. I had a '66 Chevy back then, and things I wanted to say.

Afterthoughts and Acknowledgements

Of course much is missing here. In trying to keep it concise and focused, I leave out the lyrics my childhood friend Fred Buffum and I worked on during that beautiful fall of '87. Fred and I had performed together a few times in grade school and later he was the lead guitarist in the first version of our punk band Damage during my junior year at Trinity College. Fred and I go way back to when as twelve year olds we wrote a song called "Hey Mister Seagull (What Are you Doing on the Piling?)," and if it wasn't for busy schedules, his insanely active lifestyle, and my laziness, we might have collaborated more. Who knows what lies ahead.

It's pretty obvious I'm indebted to John Laprey, Joel O'Lari, and Rob Schmoyer who helped bring my songs to life. I'll never forget Chris Chapman on drums, especially for that December session when we recorded "Terror and Love" and a handful of other more recent songs. My thanks to all the guys in Gravy Boat for showing up whenever I was in town. Chris Rose was always faithful. In more recent years I've had the privilege to play with Tobe Kniffin, who I consider a musical warrior and a kindred spirit. All of these guys are lifers, in it for the love of music.

I've kept the telling of this tale family friendly. This could have been more Gonzo in style and content, yet I didn't see a point in that. I respect people's right to privacy as much as I do free speech. Wild goings on occasionally occurred. One evening after a late night recording session, I ruined a closet full of my wife's shoes when I mistook it for the bathroom. That was an expensive mistake, but I was eventually forgiven. A younger version of me would have written a song about it, something about "My girl was not amused when I ruined all her shoes after too much whiskey in too short a time." Finding humor in the personal and making it universal is a tricky business only the masters are successful at doing. Woody Guthrie passed that talent onto son Arlo whose "Alice's Restaurant" questions a country's moral hypocrisy while simultaneously exposing its absurdity. Using wit to keep one's wits about him. Dylan's "Motorpsycho Nightmare," Prine's "That's the Way the World Goes 'Round," Twain's Huckleberry Finn. *My own sense of humor, whatever it may be, I get mostly from my mom. My dad makes friends with people from all walks of life and sometimes likes to tweak his tales. It's the telling itself that seems so enjoyable. I picked up a lot from my parents, and I keep learning as I go.*

At one point in here I mentioned the songs were mostly autobiographical. True and untrue. Even the tributes I wrote to other people were about me. An artist must be inside the work but also outside of it. I think of Blood on the Tracks *and* Astral Weeks *and the restless nature of both Bob Dylan and Van Morrison. These guys are still out there plying their trade. The music sustains them. And I think of the poet W.B. Yeats who supposedly said, "Bad artists borrow; great artists steal." I can't really explain that, but it makes perfect sense to me. Seamus Heaney's work cannot be fully digested and savored without a deep awareness of Irish culture and history, yet "At the Wellhead" and "Digging" speak more directly to me than anything from some New England poets. One who did write well and live beautifully and keep alive the power of words was Hugh Ogden whose truth and spirit still guide me. As does Bob Marley. I am not a sufferah, but Marley's lyrics speak directly to a core part of my intellect. I feel his words. And in the end, maybe someone out there might connect with and glean something worthwhile from these bits of verse. I offer them respectfully to you.*

LaVergne, TN USA
01 September 2009
156546LV00004B/35/P